GUN IN THE HILLS

By the same author

THE GUN IN THE CASE
THE FLIES IN MY HAT

Gun in the Hills

A Sportsman's adventures,
mostly in New Zealand

by

GREG KELLY

The Halcyon Press

First published 1968
by
Hodder and Stoughton

This edition published in 1995 by
The Halcyon Press
A division of
Halcyon Publishing Ltd
C.P.O. Box 360, Auckland, New Zealand

Copyright © 1968 Greg Kelly

All rights reserved. No part of this publication may be reproduced, stored in a retrieval system or transmitted in any form or by any means, electronic, mechanical, photocopying, recording or otherwise, without the prior written permission of the publishers.

ISBN 0 908685 03 3

Printed in Hong Kong by Colorcraft Ltd.

To Sportsmen

He must be active and quick eyed, well advised of speech and of his terms, and ever glad to learn, and that he be no boaster or jangler.

The Master of Game

Contents

		page
1.	The You Yang Ranges	13
2.	Pussyfooting	20
3.	The Gentle Art of Getting Lost	25
4.	I Find New Zealand	29
5.	Noble Game at Last	33
6.	The Urewera Ranges	44
7.	Mark and Invermark	54
8.	Quality in a Head	58
9.	The Wild Boar	65
10.	Trophy Tusks	72
11.	Bush Whirligigs	77
12.	Slightly Technical	81
13.	Hit the Thing!	90
14.	This Queer Madness	97
15.	"Poor Old Swan!"	102
16.	Upland Game	107
17.	"The Mallard has Saved the Grey"	111
18.	The Earthquake's Gift	115
19.	Big Duck or Small Goose?	123
20.	The Gun for the Job	130
21.	Dawn Watch for the Canada	136
22.	Kaimanawa Mountains	143
23.	Snowgrass Country	153

Illustrations

	facing page
The author in a maimai on Rotokawa water, near Rotorua	32
May 1968, Ernie Shepherd after duck	33
(*Right*): A thirteen-pointer shot by the author (*Left*): "The best fourteen-pointer I've ever seen"	48
On the Lower Retaruke River in the Central King Country	49
Boyds Rock in the mountains east of the Tongariro Park, and aircraft in which author flew out of the mountains	96
Les Mark with his pet stag and its family	97
Canada geese being driven to banding pens on Lake Ellesmere	112
River and mountain in the Haast region of south Westland	113

Foreword

We are indeed fortunate to have had sportsmen of the calibre of Greg Kelly, able and willing to put pen to paper and produce a real treasure.

Greg Kelly's *Gun in the Hills* is one of our very best hunting books. Modest, full of good stories, exciting, witty and alive, and above all a true reflection of a genuine all-round sportsman.

A book of this quality is indeed a rare gift when shared by the author with his readers. My friend Greg was no stranger to writing, having over a long period contributed to all our outdoor magazines using the name TANGATAROA which was draped over his tall shoulders by the Maori people. An honour indeed.

Greg's knowledge of firearms and their use is legendary. Having shot in the King's Fifty during the mid-twenties, he understood the finer points of rifle shooting. With a gun, his prowess was that of a well trained sportsman and a delight to watch.

As a fisherman, he was the gentleman sportsman. Exquisite in the handling of a dry fly, never really wanting to understand any other. A true purist.

For many years he was the Police Ballistics Expert unravelling many a difficult case involving firearms and his experiences in this aspect of his life are related to his finest book *The Gun in the Case*.

When asked to write the foreword for a book from this great sportsman and good friend, I felt humbled and honoured. Greg Kelly has portrayed himself perfectly in the last sentence of his introduction by saying "My final note of appreciation is to glorious New Zealand for being just what she is."

Jock Erceg
Taupo 1995

Introduction

This is a book about the sport of game shooting as enjoyed by the author, mostly in his adopted country of New Zealand. The term "gun" is used as a matter of convenience to cover all the important types of firearms referred to, whether they were pistols, rifles or shotguns.

Many sportsmen and owners of property have helped me in many ways to enjoy my shooting over the years. I take this opportunity to thank them. I am also very grateful to friends who have supplied pictures for use in this book.

I owe special thanks to the New Zealand artist Peter McIntyre for again drawing my weather-beaten person for the cover. He is indeed a very generous friend.

Once more, also, must I admit my indebtedness to Ted Webber of Havelock North for much frank advice and guidance during preparation of the manuscript and for his ever-ready help.

My final note of appreciation is to glorious New Zealand for being just what she is.

G. G. K.

Taupo, New Zealand. 1968.

1. *The You Yang Ranges*

YOU YANGS. The name fascinated me. As a child I would repeat the words to myself, over and over again without knowing what they meant: You Yangs. You Yangs.

When I grew older their meaning emerged. I became aware that the two words formed the name of a small range of mountains in Victoria, Australia; and it was near the You Yangs where my grandfather had settled with his wife and small son (my father), to establish a sheep station. I doubt if anyone else has attempted to follow in his footsteps. The old gentleman is said to have been fascinated by the dark, mysterious ranges; no reversal in his fortunes would persuade him to abandon the place and he stuck it out to the end of his days.

So it was not surprising that the name of the ranges was frequently mentioned in the family circle. I was still only a schoolboy when I finally saw the black mass at a distance of ten miles and longed to go there and explore them. I listened to tales: Gold found in the You Yangs. A man lost in the You Yangs. Police searching for a cattle thief in the You Yangs. And there was the mysterious murder of the owner of a payable gold reef, poisoned—it was said—by wild honey that he and his brother-in-law had gathered. The sensation came when it was found that the gold reef petered out to dross in retribution, the old people said, for a foul crime.

But there were other tales about the You Yangs that appealed to the hunter in me. These were about kangaroos, wallabies, foxes, wild dogs, native cats, goannas and snakes. There was an enormous black snake in the ranges, seen but rarely and named You Yang Jack, reputed to be ten or twelve feet long and as thick as a man's thigh. The memory of this yarn was to give me a bad turn on a night of terror.

It is not surprising that I took every opportunity to get away on my holidays to one of the several farms owned by my relations, especially those which were close to the You Yangs. It was from one of these, Bunjill Tap, where I went to herd sheep and shoot rabbits, that I made my first foray into the You Yangs in search of nobler game.

Bunjill Tap was not a large property, being mostly confined to a horseshoe-shaped basin with sides sloping gradually from rather high cliffs that broke away from the tableland. At one side the formation was of red volcanic rock, its face deeply eroded in places into caves. It was an intriguing hideout for foxes. The peak of this red cliff ended abruptly and made a perfect lookout over the valley.

The living quarters on the farm were simple even judged by pioneer standards. A two-roomed hut built of rough weather-boards and homemade bricks; the bunkroom had a raised wooden floor, under which an occasional snake came to live. The floor of the other room was made of crude bricks, but rabbits had burrowed under it and subsidences had meant the loss of some bricks. It was easier to fill the hollows up with clay than attempt proper repairs. No one really blamed the rabbits for this. After all, they'd had to have somewhere to get away from their own kind which reigned over all other parts of the farm. Rough as that hut was, I thought it the most desirable place in the world and was as happy as a king, especially when I was alone, as was frequently the case, for weeks at a time.

My useful weapons were a heavy ·450 revolver with a 4-inch barrel; a single-shot Winchester ·44-40 with a heavy octagonal barrel, and a ·22 single-shot Savage.

When at sixteen I joined a local rifle club I acquired a ·303 Lee-Enfield at the upset price of £3 15s. 9d. I was to pay club fees for three years at the end of which the rifle was to become my own. As this was the biggest single investment of my boyhood, and I had earned all the money myself, the exact figure is remembered.

With my new rifle and some practices at the club range, I gained confidence and some modest successes. Mr Lodge, one of the senior marksmen, carefully lined up the sights for me as well as coaching me in the art of reading the flags that indicated the force and direction of the wind, a most important matter. It is beyond doubt, in my mind, that it was Mr Lodge who gave me the skill in long-range shooting that stood to me for the next half-century.

In the next two years that I was the pannikan boss of Dunjill Tap I made many ventures into the ranges. At first these were of a minor kind as I was a bit scared by the evil reputation of the dark hills, but as time wore on and I grew older, the awe faded, helped on its way by the success of my hunting.

On one of these later trips I travelled farther than I had ever been along the foothills. There I came across a wonderful stand of bluegum saplings, whose trunks were tall and slender, running up to thirty or forty feet without a limb. The thickness was almost uniform at about ten inches at ground level. There they stood in hundreds like a crop of maize, smooth, blue, and beautiful, swaying gracefully in the slight downstream breeze. They appeared to my imagination to have been created to march across the oceans of the world like the masts in brave ships. Yet no one wanted them for this or any other noble purpose; all that could be done with them was to be cut for firewood.

Firewood! Why not? It was a chance to hit out for myself and have a camp on my own. As soon as it could be arranged I took a contract to cut the saplings down, chop them in 4-foot lengths and stack them neatly for measuring and loading.

I invested in a small tent, a camp oven and some billies, and moved to the scene of my first home.

Where I camped was in a grove of heavy messmate gums which provided me with shade, protection from storms and dry firewood. A small creek flowed, or sometimes merely trickled, behind the tent.

I was alone, except for a black retriever, still quite young, that I was training to help me in my hunting trips; also to be a good dog about camp. He had to mind his manners which he learned to do very quickly. I called him Tiger out of an inverted sense of humour, as a gentler dog would have been hard to find. Tiger had some engaging ways. When I spoke, he would assume the perfect pose of an interested listener, black curly head turned a little to one side, ears raised, brown eyes looking earnestly up into mine. The moment I stopped talking he would leap to one side, wagging his tail vigorously, and rush round in a circle as though trying to tell me that he was delighted with the idea.

I had no means of transport and had to rely on Barney, who had given me the contract, to bring my supplies from the nearest store twelve miles away. His arrival dates were uncertain and sometimes he forgot to bring them. Usually meat could be collected with a rifle, but man cannot live on meat alone. One morning I found, like Mother Hubbard, that the larder was bare. As the rifle club was due to meet the following day, I decided to take my rifle in the morning, walk to my aunt's place where a hearty meal was assured at all times, then on to shoot and pick up some stores on the way home to the You Yangs. With a bit of luck I might get a ride part of the way.

The stars were still shining as I washed in the creek, where Tiger and I had our own private baths—his downstream from mine—dressed by the fire, made a billy of tea, and left camp as daylight was breaking. The honeyeaters in the trees about my tent were just starting to chirp and flutter as Tiger and I set off on our walk.

It was a perfect morning. The longstemmed seed heads and

bluebells were heavy with dew and rapped against my shins as I swished along, and my feet were sopping wet through my cheap cowhide boots. There was some kind of herbal growth there that gave off a strong, rather sickly, odour which is not noticeable during the day. This scent rose to my nostrils as I strode along and I thrilled to its wildness. Here and there I crunched across bare patches of red clay covered by small black pebbles that looked like iron shot pellets. Banks of ground fog swirled around as though not knowing which way to go. The weird shapes of casuarinas seemed to move out of the mists in my direction, an illusion caused by my own movement, but it took a second or two to adjust one's mind to the reality. Once I was startled by a bronzewing pigeon bursting out of a wild cherry tree.

Tiger trotted behind me in his usual dignified way. The dark ranges rose like monstrous castles behind me, their rims showing tinges of pink.

There was no track to follow; I had to guess the direction and hope for the best. It was a relief, at last, to see the outline of Bald Hill against the lightening sky and know that I was dead on target. Like a pencil scratching on a slate the cries of swans overhead came out of the dark. A lone curlew piped far to my left.

It was not so very long after this that I came on the largest sheet of fresh water to be found for miles and known as the Sheepwash Dam. It was then sunrise, and rays of light tipped the ruffled water. I sat down to watch this, to me, unusual scene. All round the edges of the water was a growth of bulrushes with tall stems topped by long brown heads. Luckily, there was a break in the wall of rushes right in front of me. As I watched, a flight of diamond sparrows rose together in a cloud and took off across the plain, causing me to marvel at their complete unity of action. How do birds decide this; and who gives the signal? I looked for anything that had frightened these sparrows, but nothing showed up. An eagle was circling above the earth at, perhaps, a thousand feet, but could hardly have been the cause. It seemed they were just off on their daily affairs.

Water dams provided the only water that most farms had to keep their animals going. They were mere holes scooped out in the claypans of some depressed area. Domestic water was conserved in deep holes dug in the ground and lined with brickwork or cement. When it rained, water from every available roof was run into the "well" and the supply was always critical. But here was a huge sheet of water, acres in extent, which filled me with wonder and joy. However, its name suggested that this was not water to drink.

I was just about to move on to that needed breakfast when there was a whistle of wings right over my head and two wild ducks, the first I had ever seen, set their wings and came down on the water in front of me. It was a wonderful moment. They swam round and round, splashing and diving ecstatically. They splashed the water with their wings in what was obviously the great moment of their day.

Thrilling and all as the sight of these ducks was, the thought of food obtruded itself. Could I hit one of them? It was really an impossible shot, at least 150 yards, and a third of it over water. To get any closer was quite out of the question as they would have been off before we could move a yard. Nothing else for it but to try a shot from where I sat. There was barely any wind, as the leaves of the bulrushes showed. I had wiped my rifle barrel out ready for use before leaving camp; the sights were dead in for 200 yards. I loaded the rifle and came on aim just as I was, sitting with knees partly drawn up and heels dug into the ground. Now, with an elbow on each knee and the heavy rifle backed firmly by the shoulder, I aimed at the waterline of one of the ducks and fired. At the report one duck flew off, the other just turned upside down and spun rapidly in circles. When we reached the target area, it was dead, forty feet out.

It was then that I realised the difficulty of getting the bird out. To wade was impossible as I'd have sunk in mud to my thighs and perhaps not have been able to get out. My hope was in Tiger, who had never seen a duck and had no experience in water work, but he enjoyed retrieving sticks. I tossed in bulrush stems. These he brought out without even seeing the floating duck. I then tossed lumps of clay; they sank at once. Finally Tiger spotted the bird and swam round it twice before grasping the very tip of a wing. Then he swam cautiously out and dragged it to my feet. I examined it for wounds but there was no sign except a trickle of blood on the neck, which had been broken by my bullet!

2. Pussyfooting

All the animals in my area seemed to be gifted with uncanny wariness. To get close enough for a surekill shot made it a job calling for stealth. In that part of the Victorian bush the undergrowth was sparse under and between the big messmates and ironbark trees where the animals I sought were to be found. Matters were not improved by the slaty rock faces which made silent stalking in boots impossible.

The wariness of the animals was easy enough to understand: wallaby, kangaroo, wombat and bandicoot had been sought by the aborigines for countless centuries and had built up a survival factor that was good enough to save them from extinction at the hands of the finest hunters in the world. But I wanted wallaby and kangaroo; the skins of these two edible animals were worth money, and that was my serious need.

Though the aborigines were there in my grandfather's day they were all gone in mine, but the animals regarded me as being just as dangerous as their age-old naked enemy and kept as far out of my way as they could. The native hunter had much greater hunting skill in the first place, and was also barefooted, but I was armed with a more accurate and far-reaching weapon. So, in some respects anyway, the advantage should have lain with the rifle; but the ability to move like a shadow over ground strewn with dry twigs, leaves and slaty stones does not come naturally to a white man.

To overcome this disadvantage I had to make sneakers for my feet. Strips of sacking wound round and round the boot was one way, all right for short stalks, but the strips would work loose and start to drag at the very moment when swift and silent steps were needed. I purloined some sheep skins from my cousin's place and, shearing off most of the wool, used these to make moccasin-like boot covers, placing the woolly side down and lacing the cut edges together at the toe and on top. Their serious fault was that they did not last long and had to be replaced. As my cousin did not complain about the disappearance of his skins, and they were very cheap material for me, I used quite a few of them. The odd thing, now I think of it, is that no one ever saw me wearing my invention, nor ever found the ones I had worn out.

At my woodcutting camp in the You Yangs, I found that time was the essential thing. I couldn't give up half a day's work to looking for something to shoot for the pot, so the hunt had to be early in the morning or just before dark.

The magical moments of any day anywhere, for me, are those when the dark is losing its everlasting struggle with the light. The whole of Nature seems to be tensed with interest as the eastern skies brightened and the shadows creep furtively into the bush. It is to me the hunter's hour, the time of high expectancy, when wild creatures are moving either to or from their feeding places. Apart from the better chance of a shot, there's the queer fascination that the dawn always has for the man who finds a thrill in the first bird note of the day and can recognise the singer; and who can hear the minor music of such instruments as the rough-edged rushes leaning over his head as they're rubbed together by the first catspaw of the morning.

Every other form of life besides the hunter seems to be listening, listening and alert, so he must be as silent in his movements as he can be. When in a riverbed, as I generally was in Victoria, it was better to choose a likely spot and just sit still and wait. Oddly enough, the wallaby, and to a lesser extent the kangaroo, do not seem to care how much noise they make, so one has time to prepare for a shot. One such was offered me at a split second's notice by a band of kangaroos; they must have been pausing on the far side of a patch of light scrub to rest, or they might have suspected my being there, but I was caught completely by surprise when six or more wildly crashing bodies came flying over or through the bushes behind me. It must have been almost reflex action on my part to fling up the heavy shot ·44 Winchester and fire at a flying doe. She came down and turned end over end as I ran forward. The bullet had caught her behind the right shoulder and torn right through and she died as I reached her with a heart-piercing groan that had a human note in it. It was a thrilling shot and for a few minutes I was elated; I'd had no camp meat for some days and was glad for myself and my dog, but I felt badly about that groan. I had not heard one make any sound before and have not heard of anyone else who has. A hateful experience. After that I looked more to the wallaby and, through the expansion of my trade in skins, was able to vary the menu with some farm mutton.

I must tell of a new device that made my foot mufflers more durable and saved my cousin a number of sheepskins. One night my cousin brought home with him a strange little man who was so physically weak that my people could neither expect much work out of him, nor could they turn him away. He arrived at Bunjill in a clean shirt and trousers and a pair of blucher boots. He had a small swag and a black billycan which could not have held more than a quart. He wore no hat over his long hair, and his eyes were blue and watery as was the tip of his nose on most occasions. Everything about Harry was small, except his appetite which made up for a lot, though it did not seem to add to his strength.

One rainy day Harry was forced to take off his blucher boots and change, and I was entertained and enlightened to see the little fellow unwrap squares of flannelette from his feet. These were his "socks". Some time later in the evening, when they had dried by the fire, he put them on again. They were about the size of a baby's nappy; he simply put them on the floor, placed a foot on one of them in such a way that the big toe was pointing at one corner of the cloth, then deftly folded first the right-hand corner and then the left-hand one over the arch of the foot. He then pulled up the front corner on top of them and, ignoring the rearward corner, shoved his foot back into his boot. He caught me eyeing the proceedings and asked:

"Ain't you never seed Prince Alberts before?"

I admitted my ignorance.

"Better than socks anyday," he chuckled. "Yer see when the 'eels wear out, yer just give 'em a quarter turn. No darnin'. They larst four times the time; easier ter wash, and dries quicker. 'Sides, they don't cost nuttin' much."

I had to admit the logic of his reasoning. At the same moment I saw in a flash the solution to my pussyfoot problem. By cutting squares, a little bigger than Harry's Prince Alberts, out of grain sacks, folding them over my boots, as Harry did over his feet, and sewing them on with a packing needle and twine, I could make first-class pussyfoot wear.

A silent footfall enabled me to surprise a fox on several memorable stalks. Once, moving over the hump of a ridge, I spotted a large male Reynard looking intently into a watercourse. He was only fifty yards from me, and it was incredible that this could happen in open country, yet there he was, quite unaware of me, and he gave me a perfect shot.

On another day I was walking through dried thistles, surely the noisiest stuff possible to get through, when a fox, no doubt hunting on his own account, sprang up to the top of a rock about eighty yards off. He had evidently not heard a sound, as he stood there watching steadily away from me. I had a ·303 rifle that day, and its nine and a quarters pounds weight was perfect for steady holding for the few seconds it took to line up. I thought the bullet had missed its mark, as he sprung off the rock and raced through the thistles in a half-circle to disappear. When I reached the place where he had vanished it was to find him quite dead.

A few days afterwards I got another fox. He also seemed

half asleep, only twenty yards away, and when I fired he sank to the ground without a movement. My bullet—a ·22 this time—had hit him between the ears. When I went to pick him up it was to find that the poor devil had a trap on his hind leg. It was not one of my traps, and he must have dragged it for miles. An inglorious stalk, that was.

The art of pussyfooting became an obsession. I would spend hours practising how to move without noise, moving with bent knees on the ball of the foot and taking the trouble to wear woollen clothing that made no sound when brushed by twigs in the bush.

There were no hunting trophies in the Victorian bush to compare with the ones to be won in New Zealand. The few animals I used to stalk in those days were as children's toys in comparison with the wapiti, deer, thar, chamois and wild boars to be found in New Zealand, but I shall always be grateful to those lesser beasts in my native land for the lessons in hunting that they taught me. And although I have not had the opportunity to stalk all the bigger trophies here, I have had many years of delightful stalking for some of them.

3. *The Gentle Art of Getting Lost*

One of the luckiest days of my life gave me the first full measure of primal fear. I lost myself in the You Yangs. It was an experience I should not wish any lad to go through, for it was a six-hour period of real terror. I was closer then to death than I care to think about.

On that afternoon I went out after kangaroos. I needed meat for the camp and for my dog. As Tiger had a speargrass sore between his toes, I ordered him to stop at the camp.

My luck was out, and I found no sign of game though I'd penetrated a long way into the ranges. It was quite late when I spotted a wallaby just about ready to break, and took a quick shot at him. It bowled him over but did not stop him, and he thumped away into the scrub. To race along the valley flats was dangerous, as gold fossickers had dug deep shafts for pay dirt. All I could do was to sneak after the wounded animal and get a better shot in. Every time I got near him, he burst away, thump, thump, thump, to disappear again. It was nearly dark before I managed to put the poor little brute out of his pain and end my own distress. I gutted the carcase and straightened up.

Then I realised I had not the faintest idea which way to go to get out of the bush.

Lost people, I had been told many times, always wandered round and round in circles, coming back time and time again to the same spot. I became frightened; I missed Tiger's company. My impulse was to climb a ridge, so I did this up a steep face where slate-like stones caused me to slip and claw my way.

Reaching the top, I selected a big ironbark and decided to wait there till daylight. This was wise; but I had not calculated what fright and worry, mixed up with the local reputation of the You Yangs, would do.

Night came on. It was black dark. Then, as though at a signal, the night life of the forest woke up. There were scratchings and scutterings. Something thumped out of a tree and tore away through the dry leaves. Another followed. Two buck opossums fighting. I relaxed. Then strange sounds came to me, sounds I had never heard before. Almost the next minute, and not far away, an awful sound of groaning came to me. It was just like a man groaning with his mouth shut and his teeth clenched. The notes were short, too, with a rising scale. A cry like that of a small child pierced the night; and again came the groaning octave. Bats were flying about and making their funny little squeaks; the ghost-like voice of the boobook owl, though familiar, added to the eeriness of the night.

Then the terror of the night really struck. Some heavy animal started to move through the dry leaves close to me. It was in no hurry and seemed to move in several places at the same time. Snake! Could it be You Yang Jack?

I had never really believed that any black snake could be ten or twelve feet long, and as thick as a man's thigh. But what *was* this creeping heavy body? Could You Yang Jack be coiled up there watching me?

I could stand the strain no longer. Working my rifle slowly round in the direction of the "snake", I fired.

The bush was instantly hushed by the sound of the shot; I suppose the wild things were astonished and listening. I only remember rushing over the edge of the ridge in the darkness and slipping down the other side, slipping, slipping, and then I was in water. I sensed that this was the creek my camp was on; all I now had to do was to follow the stream down to get home.

But now stupor took over from terror.

Striking a match, I threw a leaf into the water. Immediately it was out of sight, I had forgotten which way it had gone. I tried again and again with the hopelessness of complete confusion until I was yelling with rage. I remember splashing through the water and trying to climb up the opposite ridge. It was very steep and I fell many times on the loose slate stones to claw my way up again in a mad impulse to get somewhere. I came to an opening in the forest, where there must have been some visibility, as I found myself looking at what appeared to be the wall of a large building where no building could possibly exist. Cautiously I stepped towards it and found that it was the side of a big cutting that had been dug out of the point of the ridge and that I was actually standing on a road.

I remember lighting a blazing fire against the wall of that cutting and sitting by it. My senses gradually came back to me. I became aware that I still had my rifle, but had lost the wallaby. I also became aware that I was in pain through cuts and hurts. I sat there hoping that someone would come along and help me, for I still did not know which way to go.

As I watched I noticed that someone had lit a fire away off to my left. It grew bigger and brighter. Strange, I thought, that a fire should make the sky turn white. Then, before my eyes, the moon rose, but in the wrong place! Was it moon or sun? Didn't matter. Both rise in the East. At last I became normal enough to realise that the moon must be in the right place and it was I who was wrong way about. As my camp was on the edge of the plains, and the moon rose in front of my camp, I saw that all I had to do was to go down the roadway in that direction.

Eventually I reached my camp where I was wildly welcomed by Tiger who rushed round me in excited circles making his queer "talking" noises in his throat. I was sorry that all I had to give the poor fellow was some stale scones soaked in condensed milk. After making a billy of hot tea for myself I flopped into my bunk, utterly done.

For all the battering, I had enough sense to understand how lucky I had been. I had learned some lessons that gave me bush wisdom for the next half century. Never again was I to go gawking and groping in the bush without taking careful note of my bearings; never again was I to go into the bush ill-clad, without a compass and a good stout sheath knife; never again was I to allow the fear of the dark or tales of bogies to take charge of my mind.

But for my good luck in striking that roadway, which I could so easily have missed, my case could have been just one more of "Boy Lost in the You Yangs."

4. *I Find New Zealand*

Happy as I was in my woodcutting camp in the You Yangs, I had finally to face up to the fact that, at eighteen years of age, I wasn't making much progress in life and would have to move out into the world of men.

Circumstances guided me to settle in New Zealand, and although I knew less about the country than I knew about Scotland, Africa, and the mid-West of the United States, I was soon completely at home there.

After knocking about for some months in Canterbury and the Wairarapa I decided to join the Permanent Artillery in Wellington. This was in 1906. It was as a gunner in the Force that I caught that fever for scientific gunnery and ballistics from which I have never recovered. A completely new sphere of activity and study was opened up to me, and henceforth I was never to fire a shot without set purpose and considerable respect for the powerful, accurate, and reliable weapon I was using to fire it.

But at that time soldiering was a poorly paid occupation; I could see no future in it and purchased my discharge. My love of bush country led me to a remote spot which was some hours' march from Ohakune, where a courageous man had taken up about a thousand acres of bush which he wished to have felled, fenced and grassed. Here I was to learn a great deal about New Zealand conditions and certainly about a different kind of hunting.

Our only game animals were wild pigs and wild cattle, the pigs being very much more common. The now-protected native pigeon was there in great numbers; anyone stupid enough to do so could have filled a sugar-sack in quite a short time. I soon found there was complete absence of sport in shooting these great birds. One day I missed one as clean as a whistle and the bird still sat there looking mildly down at me as though wondering what I was up to. Only hunger ever made me take another.

Our main supply of meat, when we could get it, was beef and after that the "hard-work" meat, wild pork. There were four of us in that camp. My mates were tough and highly skilled bushmen, and in their company I was soon to learn humility and, under their guidance, how to hunt with dogs. The proudest moment of my life was when these fine men invited me to join them as an equal. Our partnership lasted until they all married, when they moved off and left me; so, for a while, until I found two other mates, I chopped and hunted alone.

By this time the wild cattle had either been shot or driven to safer areas. Anyway, it would have been a shame for me to shoot a cattle beast, as only a fraction of the meat could have been used even with the help of the pickle tub.

Wherever I went I always carried a rifle or a revolver. When I had to sleep out in the bush, which happened rarely, something could be shot. I'd had the habit of carrying a revolver all my life and would have been lost without it; my favourite, though not my first, was the Webley service revolver of ·455 calibre with its 250-grain lead bullet. It is a fine target weapon as well as being (its real job) a man-stopper. Wishing to have a more compact and portable weapon I bought a ·32 Colt with a 5-inch barrel, and this was a perfect target pistol. Later I imported from the Colt factory a ·38 S & W Special which is in a class of its own both for power and accuracy.

In 1916 I started on the ·32 Colt auto-loading pistol. This was my first automatic and I was astonished at its power and penetration on porkers. Later I stepped up to a ·38 Colt auto, but was disappointed with it and returned to the ·32 auto for pigs.

After the Arms Act became effective in 1921 and it was unlawful to remove a pistol from "the curtilage of the owner's dwelling" I used a ·303 single-shot carbine with a breech adaptor which allowed the use of a ·32 S & W revolver cartridge. The full load of the ·303 is dangerous at close quarters, especially in rocky country, as fragmented bullet and flying rock matter can be blown up and around and into the shooter. It is a case of too much power being harnessed in too small a space.

Where dogs are used for pig-hunting it is necessary to get close to the pack to avoid the risk of killing a dog, and the revolver or pistol was ideal for this work.

I went out with three other chaps one day after pigs and overheard one ask another:

"Hasn't Greg got a gun?"

"Yes. He's got it in his pocket."

"In his *pocket?* What does he think he'll get with a gun in his pocket?"

The game was hard to find that day and it was quite late before the dogs gave tongue. After the usual uproar and several rushes from place to place, the animal—it was a boar—finally bailed on a steep face covered with tangled vines and wineberry. I had no trouble in getting to the scene first and was able to work my way to within a few yards without the boar's seeing and I'm sure the dogs didn't know I was there. I think I was just in time; as the animal lunged forward towards one of the pack I got two quick shots at the side of his head and both bullets went through his brain, passing out the other side. I haven't the slightest doubt that it was because I was carrying a pistol instead of a gun or rifle that I was able to get to the scene of the bail-up before the others who, by the way, were just as used to bush travel as I was.

The pistol leaves both hands free to battle through the

bush. A long-barrelled weapon is a bad handicap. It is now too late to advocate its use for target work or boar hunting, as all citizens are suspect in these unhappy days of political control. But in my bush days it was a man's right to own any arm he fancied, as long as he behaved himself. Crimes committed with guns were then very rare!

The author in a maimai on Rotokawa water, near Rotorua.
(*Photo Jeff Hamilton*)

In May, 1968, 82-year-old Ernie Shepherd was out after duck for the 73rd year in succession. At Meremere, on a lagoon near the Waikato River, he once more gained a limit bag.

(*Photo N.Z. Herald*)

5. Noble Game at Last

During my first period in the King Country, 1907–14, there were no deer of any kind. It was not until I moved to the Shannon district in 1916 that I discovered that the incomparable sport of deerstalking could be enjoyed by the humblest citizen. Hitherto I had regarded it, like the fox hunting and salmon fishing of my forefathers, as the privilege of the landed gentry. But hardly a day passed in my new environment without my hearing some yarn or other about deerstalking.

This became more so when I added guns, rifles and pistols to the stock of a business I had purchased in the town. At first I was far too busy to do much shooting, though I did manage to get in some pistol practice nearly every day. I even set up a target for ·22 pistol work in my workshop, but only for my own use and after business hours.

In the then thriving flax-milling town my business was doing very well and for the first time in my life I was able to indulge myself in the fascinating sport of target shooting, importing what I needed from the Colt and Winchester companies.

Then Mr Albert Judd, who had bought a rifle from me, invited me to join him and his brother-in-law Ted Dougherty, in a deerstalking expedition. He told me there was a lodge at the game farm at Paraparaumu and that the widow of the late curator, Mrs Carlsen, would board us at reasonable cost. I could not resist the temptation.

Everything went according to plan and we survived the trip along the winding narrow clay cattle track that led over the range from the main road to the game farm. The old widow looked after us very well, the weather promised to be fair, and we looked happily to the next morning, the first day of the stalking season.

We left the cottage as soon as we could see a few yards and I cut away north to the left side of the valley. The others, who were experienced to some degree, moved off in the opposite direction. I was, as I wished to be, alone.

In spite of my two years of motorbike riding, I was pretty fit and found the hills fairly easy going. The country was more or less open, with ferny ridges, patches of pasture and deep steep-sided gullies with thick and tangled undergrowth on the lower parts and in the bottoms.

I suppose I made every bloomer of the new chum's repertoire on the first two days and had determined to be more observant in future.

Mr Albert Judd senior joined the party on the third day. He was of tough pioneer stock and conservative tastes. He swore that his old Snider carbine was better for stags than any of our newfangled shiny ones, a view with which I could not agree, but Mr Judd was not a man to argue with. For me this was just as well.

The four of us set out next morning with the intention of two men working each side of the stream. But all my life I had hunted alone whenever I could, so it seemed natural on this occasion for me to be lagging behind the others. These men seemed to have no respect for the hearing powers of the deer tribe and barged away in their heavy boots regardless.

Finally I sat down on a small mound where a tree had once been uprooted and scanned the hillsides on my left. My heart jumped as I saw a stag come over the ridge and stand staring in my direction. The distance was only 150 yards. I counted his points carefully, I could see five on the right antler, but the other was not quite clear of the scrub.

Being unaware at that time that antlers did not always match each other, I thought the head was a legal one with a reasonable spread.

As he was facing me, I held on his chest and pressed the trigger.

Instead of falling as expected, the animal plunged down hill straight at me. Was he charging? As he came I fired twice more, but the only effect was to divert him slightly to his left. It was plain that he was done for and about to fall when a shot roared out behind me. Mr Judd's old Snider had spoken. The huge bullet hit the dying beast on the right shoulder and knocked him flat.

"What did I tell you, Kelly?" roared the pioneer. "Your flash rifle couldn't kill him in three shots. My Snider is the boy! But of course, Kelly, it's your head."

I was wise enough to say nothing except to congratulate the old gentleman on his excellent marksmanship.

Albert and Ted came running back. On looking at the head the former remarked, "It's only a nine."

"But, Albert, I counted five on his right antler!"

"Yes. They are still on, but only four on the other one." This was another disappointment. Before I had time to moan about this I heard Albert call:

"Dad. Where did you fire from?"

Mr Judd pointed out the impression of his right knee in the earth.

"And where were you, Greg?"

I went back to my mound and sat in the exact spot. Albert then took a line from where his father had knelt to where the stag was when the Snider bullet hit him.

"That bullet must have been within inches of your head, Greg," he said.

So perhaps I had been luckier than I knew.

I reported myself to the society for having inadvertently broken the rules and shot a stag with less than the legal number of ten points. Rangers Willson and Bould called to see the head at my home, but did not take it away. They said it was quite a good trophy.

The rangers also asked if they could examine my rifle. I handed it over expecting them to take possession of it. But they were only interested in what was to them a new type of rifle.

At this point I have to admit that Mr Judd was partly right in his contention about his rifle's superiority, as mine was not suitable for stags. It was the new Winchester autoloader in calibre ·401. The makers claimed that they had made it for soft-skinned dangerous game, the cat tribe — puma, jaguar, leopard, tiger. My ·401 with its 200-grain softpoint blunt bullet had an initial velocity of about 2,200 feet per sec. and an energy of 2,150 foot pounds. It was not superior to the old ·303 rifle with Mark VI ammunition which had about the same ballistics values. On the other hand it had the advantage of being able to deliver five paralysing blows in three seconds; the old bolt-action repeating rifle, even in experienced hands, needs five seconds per shot.

My mistake was in using soft-nosed bullets that burst almost on contact, whereas with a tough animal like the stag I should have used hard-nosed bullets.

The Council of the Society discussed my confession, expressed appreciation of my action in reporting the matter and allowed me to retain the head. There was no prosecution.

So ended my first season of stag hunting.

Later that same year, after the season closed, I was invited by the rangers of the Wellington Acclimatisation Society's deer farm at Paraparaumu to assist them to capture two stags and two hinds which were to be taken by the Tourist Department to the Taumarunui district for the establishment, for the first time, of a new herd.

The deer were confined to a large area of broken country that lifted up on one side of the valley from the bed of a small trout stream that runs along the valley floor. This large area of rough country was ringed by a high deerproof fence. Deer were bred there for the Tourist Department and even for zoos.

The method used to capture the animals was much the same as that used for wild horses. Adjoining one corner of the paddock there was a high walled enclosure, that had itself been divided into suitable pens. A narrow "crush" about two feet wide and six feet long was built at one side of the main pen. A deer could not turn in the crush. Stout rails, slipped in behind him, held him securely.

When I arrived at the farm by motorcycle, I found the rest of the party there. Instead of meeting only the rangers, Messrs W. Willson, C. H. Bould and W. Cobbledick, I also met Mr W. Vickery of Levin and Major R. A. Wilson, D.S.O. of Bulls. A few years later the major was in charge of probably the greatest collection of stag heads ever displayed—the sixty trophies sent to the New Zealand Court at the Wembley Exhibition in 1924.

A permanent record of these heads appeared in *New Zealand Heads* published by Country Life. Only 500 were printed and it is now a collector's piece. A copy was presented to me by the Minister of Internal Affairs with a note saying it was the last copy available.

The rangers had already hunted a number of animals into the deer pens. These included two young eight-point stags, a few spikers and a dozen hinds. It was from this lot that the officers intended to take their breeding stock for distribution. Their task would have been simple but for the presence in the main yard of a fully developed twelve-pointer which was in no mood for handling. This stag was so outstanding that he hardly appeared to belong to the party. Not only was he bigger and heavier than the two eight-pointers, though he was the same age, but his antlers were of vastly superior quality, both in weight of bone and in size.

I could not take my eyes off him, and I noticed that Major Wilson was watching him intently as if he had a personal interest in the big fellow.

Finally, I asked ranger Willson about the big stag. He answered that it had been "imported" from the Otago herd to improve the heads in the Wellington district, which were getting poorer and poorer.

By this time I had become sufficiently keen to have learnt that the original strain of all North Island deer was the park strain from Woburn Abbey, Warnham Court, and Windsor Park. This strain had been boosted by deer brought over from Australia—the Werribee Park deer.

Here in front of us was a further booster.

"We'll tell you more about him later", continued ranger Willson. "Just now our worry is to get him out of the pen, or he'll kill these young ones."

At that moment, the animal—they called him Otago—ripped open the neck not of a stag but of one of the hinds. He obviously was becoming dangerous.

The outer gate to the paddock could be pulled open quickly with a long rope; it was closed by gravity. The plan was to cut the big stag out from the others, drive him towards that gate alone if possible and liberate him.

Excitement mounted as ranger Bould got down into the pen among the deer and started to wave a length of tea-tree bush at the stag. It was while this was going on that Vickery came to grief. He was sitting on the top rail of the deer yard, just balanced there, with his legs dangling down inside. He was roaring with laughter at the antics of his friend, Bould, shooing the stag, when the big animal suddenly charged the fence immediately below his legs. In trying to draw up his feet to escape, poor Vickery lost his balance and fell backward to the ground a good eight feet below. Vickery was no longer in the flush of youth. He must have weighed sixteen stone and the fall might have killed him. As it happened, he soon recovered his breath and, although he took no further part in the circus, he later was able to walk to his car without assistance.

When work resumed ranger Bould returned to his risky job of cutting out. He had hardly started when the big stag seemed to understand what was wanted of him, and started to walk towards the gate. Cobbledick pulled the rope and all of us had begun to think the worst was over, when the big stag turned like a cat and charged the ranger who was almost in the middle of the pen. But Bould was not only a brave man. He was cool-headed. He dodged sideways into the crush, just making it as the antlers crashed against the narrow entry. The antlers were too wide and the crush too narrow, so the stag was unable to have revenge upon the enemy.

Whether it was the blow against the posts or the satisfaction that he had chased his enemy away, I do not know; but the big stag turned and walked out of the still open gate as quietly as a cow out of her bail.

Almost as though it had been stage managed, a ten-point bush stag came walking down the hill towards us. The rangers were astonished. They had never seen this stag before. This surely was a case of love defying locksmiths. The intruder had managed to get through the deerproof fence and was going to demand his rights. Theoretically, the rutting season was over, but wild animals have their own ideas on such matters. This fellow was still seeking hinds, but he was to pay dearly for his adventure.

The Otago stag was still enraged from the indignities he had suffered and charged the intruder with a savage grunt. The newcomer was a well-grown ten-pointer, he had a young appearance and evidently was quite ready to fight. The big stag's challenge was promptly accepted and there, within two hundred yards of the drafting pens, was staged an exhibition of ruthless savagery.

Both broke into a short gallop and crashed together head on. The wild stag had the advantage of being uphill, and for a few seconds seemed to be pushing the other back. The hooves of both were forced into the soil and turves flew in all directions as they pushed and twisted. Soon Otago's extra weight told and the stranger gave ground. Each was trying to get in a side-thrust at the other, but when they disengaged it was only to crash together again immediately.

We saw that the wild stag was weakening. Such fury could not last. Then Otago drew back, leaping aside, and as the other surged forward the big fellow got his chance. With a tiger-like spring forward he drove the 10-inch curved brow tine of his right antler into the other's kidney area. This would surely have been enough, but the big stag made a quick twisting motion first to the right and then to the left with that brow tine still forced right home. The damage done to the victim's kidneys and intestines was terrible.

A poignant sympathy for "that poor bankrupt" was felt by us all. He slowly moved back up the hill down which he had marched so jauntily to battle only a few minutes before. He knew his fate and accepted it as naturally as he had accepted the chance to fight for a female. The victor knew the battle was over; he stood stockstill and watched his enemy off. We saw the dying stag pause near the top of a small ridge and turn to look back. When he saw that he was still in sight of the other he seemed to make a supreme effort to struggle on a bit farther. He looked back once and, seeing then that he was out of sight of Otago he slumped to the ground. Quite plainly the last of his strength was used up in an effort to get out of the victor's sight before he fell down. When we got there a few minutes later he was quite dead.

As Major Wilson desired to have the skin, the rangers took it off for him; and it was then that we saw the fearful damage that a stag's tine can do in a fight of this kind. The whole kidney area was a mass of pulped flesh, the main paunch was torn open and the stomach was full of blood.

As we approached the scene the big stag bolted up the hill and the last we saw of him that day was on top of a hillock etched against the sky, where he made a grand picture.

Our party went back to the yard and finished the job. I learned one more thing about the stag when I tried to lasso one so that we could cut off the antlers. Though no great hand at throwing the loop I had practised the art on yearling bulls and horses with some success so I confidently offered to rope the stag. Tying the bowline and making the running noose was the work of a moment; but to throw it over the antlers and pull it back was something else again. Care was necessary not to get the loop round the beast's throat or he could be choked to death; so only the antlers had to be caught. What a circus! As soon as the rope touched an antler he gave a flick with his head and sent the loop flying up in the air again. In the end it was more by good luck than skilled roping that a loop held on one of the antlers. Hauling him to the fence, we sawed the horns through just above the burr; by this time the loop thrower was hot, red faced and much deflated, with a deep respect for a very clever swordsman.

An odd sequel to these events came in Taringamotu valley near Taumarunui in 1926. Then, as a member of the council of the Auckland Acclimatisation Society, I was asked to examine the herd which the Tourist Department's ranger, Mr Cobbledick, had established.

A letter had been received from the Minister of Internal Affairs, asking that this be done, as farmers in the district were complaining about the damage caused by deer.

The first impression was that deer should never have been liberated in that rapidly developing farming area. Mr George McIlroy took me to his dairy farm and pointed out a field of turnips. "I was relying on this crop for my cows," he said. "I counted thirty of your herd of deer on it one morning. You can have the lot back again, as far as I am concerned."

Quite a third of the crop was eaten out, much of the rest trampled with hundreds of the roots torn out of the ground. Here was the answer to the minister's question.

Mr McIlroy showed me a skull and antlers: "I found that bloke dead in my paddock last year."

The head was of a heavy nineteen-pointer, indicating that he had had plenty of nourishing food in his day. Though the size and weight were good, I was a bit dismayed at his park-deer characteristics. No sign whatsoever of Otago breeding in him.

"I'd like to get him mounted," the farmer said, "but I'm told no taxidermist will do the job unless there is a licence tag attached, or he could be prosecuted. I suppose I'd be run in too."

This matter was fixed up when the council of the society agreed that he should be allowed to keep the head and have it mounted if he wished.

I do not know what became of the head. Mr McIlroy, his wife and three of his children were tragically killed on the Ongarue railway crossing a few weeks later.

I stalked twenty stags at that place and shot five. Two were thirteen-pointers of park type, old fellows that had seen better days and, no doubt, had worn nobler antlers. Strangely enough, one of them bore the earmark made at the game farm years before.

. A good head of fifteen or sixteen points gave me a lot of exciting stalking for two days, but he beat me completely. My last glimpse of him was when he strolled into a tangled mass of lawyer vines and supplejack. There he roared and grunted. And though, in the end, only a few yards divided us, it was quite impossible to see him. Nothing I could do would coax him out.

Short of firing a blind shot, which would have been useless and stupid, nothing more could be done. Darkness fell as I sneaked back out of the undergrowth. He was still roaring at intervals, quite unaware, I'm sure, how close the rifle had been.

I should have liked a close look at this fellow in good light. From the distance at which I had seen him, he had heavy round beams with long brow and bez (bey) tines of the Scottish stag.

Since then some splendid heads of Scottish type have been shot in the Taumarunui district (Central King Country) and we know that Otago's blood had asserted itself.

6. The Urewera Ranges

The Galatea red deer herd was established by the Government Tourist Department on the fringes of the Urewera country, and it was in this area that I had the pleasure of stalking with Dr Carrick Robertson and with Mr F. C. Mappin, who turned out to be the best campmate I ever had.

Mappin and I set off first and made our way from Rotorua across the Kaingaroa Plains to the Kopuriki homestead of Dr Robertson's friend, Mr J. Grant. The plain was then a wild and desolate place to traverse. The "road" wound and twisted for sixty or seventy miles through clumps of monowai and tussock, and it seemed to us that the word "desert" would have been more descriptive. Enormous pine forests cover the greater part of this plain now, supporting the Dominion's papermaking industry.

We crossed the Rangitaiki River in a bosun's chair that ran along an overhead wire rope when you pulled hard enough. We were made very welcome at Kopuriki by Mr Jim Grant, Miss Grant, his daughter, and Ian, his son. We established our base camp on the banks of the Horomanga. The stalking licences had been picked up in Rotorua and allowed us to take two stags each of not less than ten points, and two hinds each for meat. Whoever designed that licence must have thought we were hungry.

Going to a good deal of trouble we built a very comfortable camp. The tent, an 8 × 8 centre-pole, was pitched above high-water mark, in case of flood, among a grove of tapukahi which gave some shelter. We built a curved back to the fireplace with stones which made a break for the cooking fire from the puffs of downstream air. We were quite close to the steep hills which led up to the main range, while along the bottoms of the ridges some fairly easy walking was possible over undulations. The bush above us in the roughest parts was thick and held some heavy trees and the gulches were densely scrubby.

Just after daylight we set out together for our first stalk along the river flats, scanning the ridges which rose steeply on both sides of the stream. Deer sign was not as plentiful as we had expected, and we did not see any deer for an hour or so. It was Mappin who saw the first one, a stag lying on a narrow ridge on a natural lookout from which he had a full view of the river bottom where we were. My telescope showed him up a well-balanced twelve, though not more than about 36-inch length by the same width. The tines showed up well as of good length and even quality. At the time we spotted him he was lying down facing, and no doubt watching, down the ridge. When I roared he sprang to his feet, ran round in a circle and roared back. We were out of his vision sitting among wild briars. Oddly enough there were no hinds in sight, an unusual circumstance. Only twice on his advance down the ridge did he show himself, and he put in at least half an hour sneaking the half-mile. He roared a few times and sounded more savage each time, but he bawled when he was out of our sight. The answers he got were only just enough to keep him coming. My mate sat in silence and I had the feeling he had not seen this sort of show before, though he had a successful trip to the Rakaia.

Then the stag was standing in full sight without the slightest sound. Mappin saw him before I did, but made no move to shoot. Then there happened one of those silly things that are inseparable in shooting:

"Go on, Mappin, go on, bust one at him."

"No, you shoot."

The stag would be gone any moment. They don't stay long when looking for an enemy and he could get our scent any minute. That minute came in a flash. He spun half-round and I thought he was lost but my mate's rifle spoke and the animal stumbled and rolled off the ridge out of sight. I ran as hard as I could the hundred yards to the spot and Mappin followed. When we got there it was to find the beast on its side on top of a tangled mass of bush vines. We could not see what sort of head he had and I was moving forward to try to lift the head when I saw that the eyes were tightly shut, a sure sign that he was conscious, though perhaps badly wounded. As I had my rifle in my hands I fired straight into the heart area. A convulsive jump and some violent kicking resulted. In a few seconds all was still and the eyes remained open. I had not seen a red deer act like this, though it is said to be common with wounded fallow. As I turned to shake hands with my mate he remarked quietly: "Thanks to you."

Dr Robertson joined us next day and during the time he was with us was lucky enough to shoot a twelve-point stag. This called for a celebration and we had a jubilant lunch when we got the head and cape back to camp. Late in the afternoon I started to skin out the head and neck, as the doctor said he wished to get it mounted. While I was at work he came out to watch me.

"Kelly," he said, "let me do some of that."

"No thanks," I answered, "I'm used to this job." I was really afraid that he might cut himself.

"But look," he persisted, "I'd very much like to do some of the work."

I was about to refuse again, a bit sharply, when I suddenly remembered that I was speaking to a famous surgeon. Then followed an experience that is still clearly etched on my memory. As soon as he got the knife in his hand the man was complete master of the situation; instead of flaying the skin from the flesh, as I had been doing, he started to separate and examine the muscles.

"You see this long flat one here?" he said. "That's the platysma, and it's the one a horse uses to quiver his skin to dislodge a fly. And this great one—see how it fans out at the end?—must be the strongest in the beast; it's one of two that carries the weight of the head—he uses it for the quick upward thrust of his antlers; terrific power there. And here's the artery . . ."

I watched the rather short, strong, white fingers as they worked and explored. The razor-sharp knife moved quickly, sometimes flat on its side, like a living thing: yet it must have felt a clumsy enough instrument to the operator. This was a wonderful thing to see; the hands were not still for a second and swift, strong, assured.

Then a terrifying thought struck me like a blow. Would those strong white fingers ever have to do this sort of thing inside my own body? I lost the thread of what the doctor was saying. I felt cold and sick. Nor do I now remember who finished the job on that stag's head. Almost exactly thirty months later, my strange foreboding became fact. An orange-sized growth developed on a lung and had to be removed by surgery. There was only one man in the world for me. Those same masterly hands, in a dozen or more major operations over a period of twelve months, carried me through and gave me strength to recover.

I, too, had shot a stag; but it was not a good one. We had needed meat. It came to the last day and I had resigned myself to looking back on another unsuccessful season, when I spotted a stag about half a mile away on the side of a steep hill. He had one hind with him and was travelling at a steady walk away in a northerly direction. The telescope showed that he was a takeable head and I called to Mappin to get his rifle. We ran as fast as possible in the direction of a small knoll that terminated the outer ridge of the range. As the deer were on the second ridge and there was a gully in between, we had a good chance of getting to the knoll before the deer, without their spotting us. The matter was very urgent and, as I had a slight start of my mate and was wearing light rubber shoes, I got to the knoll first. Half a mile run slightly uphill was quite enough to leave me gasping for breath and with a heart belting like a trip-hammer. When I got near the top of the knoll I threw myself prone and wriggled up to peep over the rim. There I saw with dismay that the animals, hind leading, had passed the point where I expected to see them and were almost in line with my "wind". At any second they would get the "man smell" and be off. I was almost cooked and in poor shape to take the shot yet there was no time for recovery. Suddenly the hind stopped and swung completely round facing the stag. He threw up his head and I saw the antlers jerking from side to side. Two jumps above and they would be over the ridge, so the shot had to be taken at that moment. I drew a bead on the hill above the stag and, holding my breath for a second or two, I pulled the sights downward. As they were passing the stag I fired and saw the animal collapse. So did I, and there I stopped, still gasping and shaking for a few minutes. My mate got to the stag before I did. When I joined him it was to see blood running from the knuckles of his right hand. He had fallen when running. This was distressing to me, but he took no notice of it.

"Kelly," he asked, "when you sent me the other side of the knoll, how did you know that if the deer saw you they would run back past me?"

I said I didn't know.

"Well," he said, "the hind did; in fact I could nearly have hit her with my rifle barrel."

The stag had fallen dead in a washout. When we dragged him out it was to find a good royal of thirteen points. I found that my bullet had struck the base of the neck. What a fluke!

Considering my condition, and that the stepped distance was 260 paces (the air line perhaps fifty yards less), it must be agreed, I think, that this was one of those game shots which Stewart Edward White in his *Land of Footprints* says is "accepted with gratitude".

(Left): A handsome thirteen-pointer shot by the author in the Urewera mountains in April, 1927. *(Right)*: "The best fourteen-pointer I've ever seen."

(Photo: Jeff Hamilton & G. C. Seccombe)

Grand country for pheasant: On the Lower Retaruke River in the Central King Country.

(*Photo J. Erceg*)

We left camp next morning with all our camp gear and five heads piled on to a dray which Mr Grant sent up for us. All this had to be chaired across the Rangitaiki and reloaded in or on to the Buick. We'd had a happy and fairly successful season. We called at a spot near the Huka Falls where a warm spring provided us with hot mineral baths. We had a few days fishing in the water that was afterwards to become world-famous. We did not fish for limit bags but we collected some good ones, including a 12-pound cock fish and a 9-pound hen. It was with reluctance that we finally made our way home. A rather strict road inspector, a native of England who had once been cook to the Scott Expedition, booked us for doing thirty-seven miles an hour on the Matiakau Road and stated in evidence that we had a "boondle of faggots" on the carrier. Fancy describing five good stags' heads as a bundle of faggots! Fined seven pounds.

We made a second trip to the Urewera Ranges in the following stalking season but met many mishaps. The first of these fell on our neck on the first stage of our journey from Auckland to Rotorua, where we had planned to stay the night. The engine of the Buick seized up near the village of Pokeno. A mechanic there said that the matter was serious and could take several days to rectify. Back in Auckland at the garage the foreman said that, in his opinion, the job could not possibly be done overnight. Mappin put me to bed in his home at about ten o'clock. He then went back to the garage workshops to watch the hardworking mechanics fighting against time to put matters right. The indefatigable F.C.M. came back in the early hours, roused me out, told me that it was a makeshift job but that it was worth taking a chance. I tried to dissuade him, saying that I'd be glad to cancel my leave and we'd go when the car was really above suspicion. It was no good.

"It's my job to get you there," he said. "I'll do it if it costs me a hundred pounds." I recalled his family crest, a charging boar—*cor forte calcar non requirit* (a stout heart requires no spur). That was it! I also understood why England wins her wars. Nothing will stop the blighters.

So we piled in and away we went again. It was not very long before the engine started to sing its death-song again. So there we were. A taxi was called for and engaged to get us to Rotorua, where the driver dropped us in the public park and refused to go another yard. We bedded down on a couple of benches under some trees, clothes and all. Before we got down I took the precaution to advise Constable Mallabond, whom I knew, who we were and not to run us in as vagrants. He didn't. I don't know whether Mappin slept or not. He was away looking for another taxi when I left my virtuous couch and staggered to the fountain for a wash.

In time M came back with the news that he had found another aged hero who did a bit of taxi work. What he paid for this job I wasn't told, and it would have been tactless to ask. In the course of time we bumped into the police-station at a place Mapp. kept calling Fartditi, but was really Te Whaiti. There we were given a good meal by the constable's wife, who was also district nurse. When we asked the constable, Mr Macpherson, about the road ahead, he said, "It's narrow and twisty but not so bad. Look out for a mad trucky. Shoot the b—— if you like. He's your only danger."

We met the b—— on a bend. He had three long shear-legs of 8 × 8 hardwood that stuck out at an angle and projected about eight feet in front. The three went right through our car and stuck three or four feet out the back. By a bit of luck the three of us had squeezed into the front seat, but anyone in the back seat would have been pretty badly hurt. The nearest baulk of timber entered the car just behind the old driver's elbow, so we in the front got off scot-free. We finally limped along in the twisted car to Ruatahuna. Our guide George met us with horses and we were soon under way. The bush track went through native forest along sidings and over streams; once or twice we travelled down steep and narrow ridges. Rain fell in heavy showers, but there was comfort in the thought that the gear and supplies were packed to provide for these conditions. It was nearly dark when we reached the guide's house. Two small children watched our approach and then, with a startled "Pakeha, Pakeha," scuttled into some bushes.

Mrs George had a hot meal ready for us, and we were quite ready for it. The room was a large one and everything was clean and tidy. There, for the first time, I saw a whole floor covered with a single mat made of plaited flaxleaves. The diamond pattern was as regular as though it had been made with a machine. No ends or edges could be detected and no dye had been used. The colour was that of wheaten straw, and the whole thing was beautiful. It made one wonder how much of this sort of native art has been lost by our Maori people. I had been in many Maori homes in the North Island, including Great Barrier, but not anywhere had I seen such as this. Small bits and Maori kits, yes, but to see the floor of a large room entirely covered was an experience that has not since been repeated. Mapp. put up the tent while I was gassing inside; he's an expert at this job, and fixed the bunks for which, like the meal, we were well ready.

It was a stormy night, the tent cracked and tugged at the guys, but everything held and we slept until daylight. George saddled only two horses this time as M refused a mount and walked the whole way and carried a good load too. I chivvied him a bit in an effort to get him to ride, but it was no use.

"Kelly," he said, "I wouldn't have ridden down that steep ridge, as you did yesterday, for a thousand pounds."

We were heading for a valley the Maori called the Parahaki. In the afternoon, when told we were about far enough, I picked a level spot by a small stream. A grove of young tawa trees gave the place a pleasant setting and as tawa burns well even when it's green we were assured of plenty of firewood. The trip was better than expected. Our only mishap that day was when the pack-horse bolted, and when we recaptured the trembling foam-covered beast it was to find that some of our gear was a bit worse for wear. My duffel bag was ripped in three places and our tucker took a beating, especially the three dozen eggs. It was just as well they were packed in a tight billy and though every one was broken, they were still with us: it's true they were then egg pulp mixed with paper, and our omelettes needed picking over a bit to get the shell and paper out.

In spite of the frost setting in with a mean hand, our guide would neither eat with us nor sleep with us in the tent. He also refused the jolt of whisky we considered he had earned. He made up a bed of fernleaves by the fire and covered himself with a single blue blanket and slept in his clothes. We were chilly enough in our good sleeping-bags, as we must have been about 3,000 feet above sea-level.

When I got up in the morning it was to find George sitting up examining a bloody toe.

"What's happened to your foot, George?"

"A *kiore* bit me."

"A rat bit you? What, here?" I asked. "What did you do?"

"I kick him and he go away."

I had a look at the toe and saw a double chisel cut with a strip of skin between. It seemed incredible that rats would be in this remote place but they were there all right. I saw one running along the edge of a pool, and there were footprints galore. The rat was the Norwegian variety, which goes to show the ability of this enemy of mankind to spread across country and survive, even prosper, in the primeval forest as well as he does in the city grain-store or sewer.

George outlined the lie of the country and how the ranges ran, then we split up. I took myself almost straight up the range opposite the camp where I had heard a stag roar half-heartedly through the night. M went with George downstream to where there had once been some attempt at making a farm, and came back with the following story:

"We'd just come in sight of a sort of clearing when George sat down suddenly. Not seeing anything and not knowing what he was up to, I sat too. We just sat and sat. No talking at all. After a long time I got a bit sick of it and said, as there was nothing there, hadn't we better move on. The Maori looked surprised and then pointed: 'Tere some deer.' 'Where?' 'Tere. Just tere'. I looked and looked. Then I saw them— a hind and stag, and then two more hinds. They'd been standing there all the time. George had spotted them and then, assuming I had done so too, had squatted down for me to make up my mind what I was going to do."

"What *did* you do then?"

"Nothing. The stag had only about six points."

We let the guide go home that afternoon with orders to come back in five days.

We each killed a stag and they weren't so bad either, fairly balanced twelves, but the timber was not heavy, and it seemed hardly worth the trouble we would have to get them out of that blasted place as we'd have had to lug them a fair distance back to camp. From there we would have had to trust them to that crazy pack-horse, if he would accept them, which was doubtful. So regretfully we left them in the bush. We had seen plenty of deer, all reds, but the stags all seemed to be dressed with light antlers. Not one rugged head was spotted during the whole time.

We had been told that this was virgin country where no one had ever stalked before. We could well believe it.

7. Mark and Invermark

The best head that I have seen carrying all the characteristics of the Otago strain was shot by Mr L. S. Mark of Taumarunui in 1941. As this head has made North Island stalking history, the story is best told in the stalker's own words:

"It was in 1941 when I was nineteen and I was crosscutting in the native bush. It was nine miles by jigger, a Model 'A' Ford truck, on rails to logging operations. We had 35 chains of steel rope out from a Williamette hauler and were feeding this with a D-7 tractor for a radius of 25 chains.

"I tried to get away (to the war), but the manpower board in Wanganui refused, saying I could not be spared from this essential work. I was not allowed a day off, even when the boss rang them for me.

"As the stags were starting to roar, I took my ·303 rifle to work one day, and after work was done I headed after the stags, but could not get on to any that night. I had a couple of sandwiches over from my lunch, covered myself over with a couple of old coats at the hauler, and went to sleep. It was a cold night of heavy frost.

"No stags roared till about 7.30, about the time the men were due. After some hesitation, I struck down and across a gorge and followed the sound of the stags which were then going well. Some half-dozen hinds kept moving on after the boss stag who would roar occasionally and then, after complete silence for a minute, the lesser ones would start to roar.

"So up and on up the ridge they went till after eleven

o'clock, when I moved closer. The stags got more and more worked up. First one and then another would let go. Then finally one went right in challenging the boss equally violently.

"Suddenly, I heard their antlers clashing; and realising they were in battle I ran right in among the hinds, which broke in different directions, till I saw a sight I can still see after more than twenty years. Two great stags in mortal combat in a small 'bull-ring', a clearing on a hill-top. They were locked together heaving and straining for an opening to get in a quick upward thrust in the flank. One would give a great push and the other would give ground in quick jumps, then with a mighty effort would throw the other back.

"Seeing that they could not go on much longer without one or the other being gored or tines broken (I found that the twelve had already broken a tine) I stepped in to about 25 feet and shot the bigger one, through the shoulders. He gave a great grunt and gave ground; but the other one, a big twelve-pointer, got into him again and was heaving his mightiest when I shot him in the chest. Both of them parted, walked about a chain and dropped dead."

In a footnote at this point Mr Mark says: "I'll finish this later. This has been lying round here for a month."

I've not yet received the rest of the story in writing, but can recall his account of the events which followed.

The "boss" was a fourteen-pointer and the other was a twelve. It was also a very fine trophy, in spite of the broken tine; but the hunter could carry only one head out of the bush. He tells me that though he searched for the other stag's head many times he was never able to find it nor even locate the scene of the fight.

When he returned to the hauler the following day he was not very cordially received and was told he was "on the skids". The bush boss asked him if he had got anything.

"Yes, I got one."

"Any good?" (The boss was a capable stalker himself.)

"Yes, not bad."

"What did y' do with it, Les?"

"Aw, I planted it in the bush."

"Mind showing it to me?"

"No, so long as I can keep it."

"Of course, Les. It's yours."

So the mighty trophy was dragged out.

"Les, I'll give you a fiver for that head."

After some days the head was handed over, and the boy took his money. It was to be many years before he saw that head again.

Then, one day, when deep in the bush on a stalking trip, Mr Mark met another hunter who was a stranger to him. After normal greetings from one sportsman to another, the stranger asked:

"Aren't you Les Mark?"

"Yes."

"I thought you might be. Larrett is my name. You're the man who shot that big fourteen at Taurewa aren't you?"

"Yes."

"Would you like to get it back?"

"Ah," Mark said, "I'll never get it back; but I'd give a hundred pounds to get it again."

It was then that he learned that a European doctor had it in his Auckland consulting rooms. Perhaps if he heard the story he might release it. Though the doctor was sympathetic, he would not part with the trophy; but he made Mark a promise that if ever he left New Zealand he would reconsider the matter.

The doctor was as good as his word and rang Mr Mark one night to say; "I'm moving to South Africa. You can come and collect your old head if you will pay me what it cost."

"I took a hundred pounds in notes," Les told me. "If the doctor wanted any more I'd have given him a cheque for the balance. But he would only accept £60 which it had cost him."

I saw this stag in Taumarunui in 1957, almost sixteen years from when Les Mark shot it. It was brought to a meeting of the newly formed Deerstalkers Association (sub-branch of Waikato) and now the Central King Country branch (N.Z.D.A.). It was amusing to watch the expressions on the faces of members as they came into the hall and saw the head. One after another they would stand and stare at the trophy and walk away.

Mr Norman Douglas himself measured this head according to the Douglas Score system, awarded it 350 points, and named it an Imperial Stag.

That this score is exceptional can be seen by the winning of the 1964 Mel Larritt trophy for the best red-deer head to be shot in New Zealand with a score of $319\frac{1}{4}$ points on the Douglas scale. It is no detraction from the latter's value to make this comparison. The man who shot this stag in South Westland, Mr A. Mackie of Taumarunui, was awarded the Orbell Trophy also, for the best all-round head of all species including wapiti taken in 1964.

8. Quality in a Head

The greatest head of red deer in existence is that which is known as the Moritzburg head. Its history has not been traced back beyond 1586, when it was first listed in the inventory of Moritzburg Castle.

W. A. Bailie-Grohmann refers to this stag in his *Sport in the Alps* and says that he was permitted to examine the old Moritzburg records in an endeavour to trace its origin, but was unable to go back any further than the date mentioned of 1586.

This information is contained in the March issue of 1950 of the *New Zealand Fishing & Shooting Gazette* (now extinct) and a photograph of the head appears on the outer front cover of the issue known as the Red Deer Record Issue.

Some idea of the size of the Moritzburg head can be formed from the spread of the antlers. At $75\frac{1}{2}$ inches (6 ft $3\frac{1}{2}$ inches) it exceeded H. J. Nitz's great N.Z. trophy of 50 inches (4 ft 2 ins) by over two feet.

The other figures of the Moritzburg stag are:

	R	L
Length of antlers	$47\frac{1}{2}$	$47\frac{1}{4}$
Points (tines)	12	11
Bay tines	$20\frac{3}{4}$	$20\frac{1}{2}$
Brow tines	22	$21\frac{1}{4}$
Circumference of brow tine	$7\frac{7}{8}$	$7\frac{1}{4}$
Burr	14	14
Beam above burr	$11\frac{7}{8}$	$12\frac{1}{4}$
Beam above bay	$9\frac{3}{8}$	$10\frac{1}{4}$
Beam above tray	$8\frac{1}{4}$	9

Weight: $41\frac{1}{2}$ lbs

The *Gazette* also reports: "This is the first time that the figures have ever been published. They were obtained by Mr Wm Gay, of Dorset, England from Dr Edwin Henslier, of Dresden Museum."

It is a pity that we have not the measurements of the trays and the surroyal tines, as with these we could have worked out the total points of value to the plan now known as the Douglas Score.

Apparently when Baillie-Grohmann saw the antlers, they were unmounted, being attached to the bare skull-bone.

We had no means of really recording points of quality in hunting trophies until Mr Norman Douglas of Waiuku, Franklin County, New Zealand came up with his plan.

As this is now the adopted system of evaluating trophies by the New Zealand Deerstalkers Association it should be explained in terms used by the author himself in the introduction to his book "*A Handbook on the Measurements of Antlers, Horns & Tusks*" which is published by the N.Z.D.A.:

"In this measuring system, the score for all the counterparted parts is the lesser or shorter measurement doubled. An inch of growth is a point of merit; an inch of non-symmetry, a point of penalty.

"The *Total Score* is the sum of these lesser scores plus whatever is taken from the evaluation of Spread and Span.

"The basic requirement of this scoring system is the recording of a pair—not a single antler, horn or tusk, but a pair. And the record is to be that trophy of the greatest symmetrical size.

"It should be appreciated that any mathematical system that is sound in principle for the recording of the symmetrical size of a pair, must give a value of nil for a single side. This is because a single side is not a pair.

"Further, a single side is not even a part of a pair. It only becomes a pair when a second side, or counterpart appears. However small this counterpart may be, this is the beginning of a *pair*. At this point, then, the *score* for a pair must begin."

It will be clear from what inventor Douglas elaborates so emphatically, that a hunter with say a big thirteen- or fifteen-pointer, would not relish seeing his trophy penalised through the loss of count on that odd tine which might be a very good one. Such a hunter would oppose the adoption of the system. It explains why Mr W. H. Robinson who was president of the association on the night of its official acceptance of the Douglas system, should say in his foreword to the book:

"For many years the Douglas System has been hotly debated at N.Z. Deerstalkers' conferences."

It was, even on the night of its adoption, a subject on which no punches were pulled by some straight-speaking, straight-shooting members. I was there. And my vote went for Douglas, whose logical and calm defence of his plan is something to recall with pleasure.

After laying down the rules for measurements the inventor added:

"No claims are made for the Douglas Score as to its exactness or perfection for 'judging' heads to the tastes of all hunters in terms of conformation to some specific shape they may carry in their mind's eye. To do so would be an impossible task, for a close study of these hunters themselves reveals as great a variation in their fancies and tastes as their trophies in conformation, strain or style."

Though the Douglas system is the only one I know that allows measurement-value comparisons to be made, forming, as it does, a basis whereby heads can be recorded and compared by mail, it has had many critics among stalkers; and this in spite of its being the officially adopted system of the New Zealand Deerstalkers Association.

Some of the criticism has been founded, I fear, on envy and much of it has been couched in harsh words. No one else, for all that, has come up with a *system* that could possibly work to satisfy a reasonable proportion of hunters.

But there is something to be said for beauty in a head that cannot gain a single point under the Douglas rule. Perhaps the idea can be conveyed in a letter which I received from the late Peter McDonald of Featherston. Mr McDonald was a famous taxidermist as far as deer heads were concerned. Some of his work was accorded highest place in the Panama Exhibition in the early years of the century. It is just chance that the head of which he writes was one of mine.

Featherston
July 5th 1927

Dear Sir,

I'll send those three heads on to you this week. Yours will go first by itself as three are too many (they don't look after them).

My object in writing to you is to draw your attention to some very special points. In the first place the skin is very uncommon; it is the lightest in colour that I have yet seen and is a *curly one*. This latter feature is a grand one, but it is unfortunately very rare. The curls are just where the neck starts *underneath*, then the whole of the neck is slightly so.

(1) Carefully examine the spot before you take off the packing.

(2) Then clean the eyes, etc., and take a rough comb and comb the neck loosely *back to front* (the lie of the hair will guide you).

(3) Comb right up to the cheeks with a *slightly forward motion* as you get back near the shield use a straight-across motion.

(4) Now with your fingers or a small brush make that little "dish" of curls come into perfect balance.

As you will disarrange it a little in the hanging up you will have to retouch it over again. Now stand off and look at it sideways and you will see the best job I have ever made of a head. The head itself is a beauty.

I remain Yours faithfully
Peter McDonald.

P.S. That head looks well at any angle but it specially took my fancy when I looked broadside on at it—it is alive.

P.McD.

I have just measured this head by the Douglas Score. It is $277\frac{1}{2}$. A mere pup.

It will therefore be seen, there can be quality in a trophy that the Douglas system just cannot recognise.

There is another value in any trophy. It is one that cannot be shared or passed on. This is the "taking or killing" value that belongs only to the man who has stalked and killed it. One could call it the memory value. For the life of me I cannot understand how any man can get much satisfaction out of being the owner of a trophy that he did not collect by his own efforts and his own personal hunting skill.

Wrapped up in the foregoing few lines is a hint of the ancient art of venery. It is an almost faded art in our country. The practical New Zealander, it is true, still stalks his deer. If he is after the "head" he takes that and moves off. If he wants the meat he guts the carcase; he rarely mentions gralloching his stag. The man who looks for reward only in taking the skin, and perhaps "a bit o' meat" has little reverence for, or knowledge of, the ancient terms which the old sportsmen used.

We of the head-hunter type stick fairly faithfully to some of the usual terms of venery. And most of us will not kill a stag that is inferior to the best of our earlier efforts. We stick to the names of tines, as each one means something to us.

QUALITY IN A HEAD

We wish for a warrantable stag; or a well-built ten-point; the next above that is the hart, a twelve-point, which, if we can take a nip of wine out of the little cup in the crown of each antler, we call a royal hart or royal stag. The daddy of the lot is an imperial stag. He has to have fourteen points, seven on each antler, in order from the burr up, of brow, bez (or bay); trez (or tray) and the sur-royals. There must be no "sport" tines or sprigs. Look at the picture of the Mark imperial and you will see a perfect example.

It is to be admitted that many of the old terms of venery are quite unacceptable to modern English. No one would be understood, even among deerstalkers, who started to blather about a royal hart proclaimed, in referring to a stag he had missed and lost; or to talk about a staggard when he meant a four-year-old stag. So, though we regret the loss or disuse of many good hunting terms, without which one once disclosed his ignorance, it is silly to try to keep useless ones alive.

Just for the fun of it, here are some of the once common names:

Of fallow deer:
    1st year — fawn
    2nd year — pricket
    3rd year — sorel
    4th year — sore
    5th year — buck of first head
    6th year — great buck

Of a doe:
A fawn; a tegg (or pricket's sister); a doe. After that, like a woman, she got no older.

According to Eric Parker, there is no authority for "imperial" as a classification for a stag's head. "Pints are imperial, not stags."

And C. E. Hare in *The Language of Sport* asks: "Could that have been better put?"

Well. This may be so, but there is some term needed for the head of more than twelve points, the royal, and surely

"Imperial" is fitting. Again, as Douglas uses it in his officially accepted booklet, it should be good enough for us.

The booklet covers all ungulate game of New Zealand: moose, wapiti (elk to Americans), Sambhar deer, fallow, Virginia (White Tail) sika, rusa, chamois, tahr, boars and goats. The booklet is enriched by drawings by the author, with some photographs to boot.

9. *The Wild Boar*

The only pigs I had ever seen before coming to the King Country were those on farms. They were all hand fed and sleekly fattened. Tame pigs, fat pigs, slow, ponderous, intelligent, with a liking for having their backs scratched, slow to get out of one's way ... I had imagined bush pigs would be just about the same, but I was wrong. The wild boar is not to be despised as a game animal in the New Zealand bush; in fact, he is the only game that is really ready and willing to tackle a man, especially when he is cornered and angry. Then he can charge with appalling speed and ferocity with a dirk in each jaw.

Apart from this exciting possibility, he is an animal which is not exactly easy to find in the bush. The best way is to use a dog, or better still, several dogs.

The original pigs were liberated by Captain Cook, some say, that he might have fresh meat when he returned on later voyages. Others assert that it was for the benefit of the natives, that they might have a change of diet. Whichever is the true version, tradition credits him with the first liberations and many people refer to the wild pigs as "Captain Cookers".

The truth is surely that early settlers took pigs to their settlements and farms. Anyone with experience of domestic breeds will agree that they are difficult to keep penned. Once out of the pen, and with nobody looking, they would take to the bush. This must still happen, as I have seen all kinds and colours of "grunters" in the King Country, far removed from the sea coast, and in the Tararua Ranges.

The rapid rise in the numbers of wild pigs should have warned early settlers and legislators about the risks involved in the liberation of animals from other countries, animals that could get completely out of control; but apparently no one worried about such trifles in those days. And, although he is called an "infestation" in official literature, he is not the worst by a long chalk.

My false idea of the wild boar nearly cost me dearly, when I met a very large and angry tusker in the King Country bush for the first time. The dogs had located him in a deep gully where the undergrowth was thick. He had not gone far when he bailed. Not knowing the game, I barged off down to deal with him. My mates, who did know the game, stopped on the top of the ridge above the yapping pack. Before I could get there, the boar broke and tore up the hill. I turned and laboured my way back uphill behind the hunt. The quarry bailed again under a tree in a mass of vines and the five dogs were raising hell's own racket in there too.

I was about gasping for breath when I got up close to the uproar. Douglas yelled out: "It's a boar, Tom, where's Greg?"

I thought: "What am I supposed to do?"

Doug called: "Look out, Greg, he might break your way!"

What if he did? These fellows must think I'm slow not to be able to get out of the way of a blooming pig.

Things happened in a flash. There was a crash, a yelp from a dog, and a great tawny and black form was sailing over a log straight for me. Instinctively, like a boxer, I side-stepped behind a rangiora bush and the beast missed me by inches as branches of rangiora lashed my face, hands and side. My mates, the Holley boys and the five pig dogs tore past.

The boar found a new fort under a divided tree. The two upper limbs, big enough for milling logs, ran side by side almost touching. Underneath he had room to manœuvre. With his stern against the upward log, and the cover of the two branch logs above, he had only the front and two sides to defend against the dogs.

Everything happened so suddenly that the kill was over before I could get over my shock and fright, and run down the track to where the hunt finished. When I did get there I was greeted with sly grins from my mates and, I swear it, grins from the dogs.

I gathered that Tom Holley had sprung on top of the double logs and fired his 12-gauge down between them. Tom's charge of shot had struck the boar above and between the shoulder-blades making one hole an inch and a quarter across. The shot shattered the animal's vitals. We dragged the carcase of the boar from under the logs. He was immense. We reckoned he was six feet long and 400 lbs in weight.

The hunt was over. So was my first lesson. The outstanding impression of that hunt, and my inglorious part in it, was the amazing agility of a wild boar. I was to forget for all time the slow, ponderous, overfed farm pigs.

In the next several years the pig-hunt was to be one of my chief sources of entertainment. Under the tutorial guidance of my friends the Holley brothers, I was soon made wise in the ways of dealing with the problems of living and working in the heavy New Zealand bush.

In every respect these men were efficient in their work and camp life. In hunting they seemed to have developed a sixth sense for locating their quarry. An instance of the latter gave me a fadeless memory.

Tom Holley and I were riding up a steep, narrow ridge top when the thick undergrowth each side of the track burst into activity. Before I could make up my mind as to what was happening, Holley dived off his horse in a smooth catlike movement into the scrub. Then there was a wailing squeal as the bushman got to his feet again with a quarter-grown pig in his arms. He was gripping the wildly struggling, squealing animal to his chest, belly outwards. All four legs were free and were thrashing the air.

All this was astonishing enough; but the comedy took a fantastic turn. By squeezing hard the man reduced the squeals to gasps but when he reduced the pressure the squeals became real again. By varying the squeezes in degree and tempo the amazing fellow was making bagpipe music and almost playing a tune.

When Holley reached for his sheaf knife I couldn't stand it.

"Don't kill him, Tom, don't kill him," I pleaded. "Poor little wretch; he's only a baby."

"What! He's a perfect porker," he answered.

"Please, Tom. Let him go," I called. "We've plenty of meat in camp. Do let him go."

"Well, I'll be damned," he muttered with a glint of anger as he spotted new pigment on his shirt; but he put the almost exhausted porker down. It lost no time staggering off after the rest of the family which was by then far, far away.

As we rode up the track still chuckling, I asked Tom: "How did you know the pig was there?"

"I didn't. I saw the sow and two young 'uns run between those two little matipos and guessed there'd be more than two following her, so I dived on the chance and this bloke ran into my arms.

I thought that over. "What if the boar had come instead?" I asked.

"No. I heard him whoofing down the side in the gully."

"Aren't you afraid of getting staked?"

"Not in uncut shrub, much," he answered.

Then he let me know the subject was closed by remarking: "I must put down another batch of bread tonight."

Where we were at that time, heavy native bush covered vast areas of the country. It was a perfect home for wild cattle and pigs. Although the general belief was that these animals were there in thousands, this was not so. We had to hunt for our beef and our pork, which took up quite a lot of time,

THE WILD BOAR

and time lost from our work meant time without pay. My old methods of pussyfooting through the bush would not do at all for pigs because the undergrowth was too thick.

An instance of this happened one day when I was without dogs and I was sneaking along slowly hoping for a bit of luck to break my way. I heard a pig rooting and snuffling somewhere within a few yards. Loading my rifle, I kept still and waited. The pig, a boar of size, moved very slowly. For a quarter of an hour or so I was so close to him that I felt my rifle barrel would touch him if I poked it through the intervening bushes. In fact, a crooked stick at my feet moved as he rooted forward. To fire at a target I can't see is something that I have never been able to do. I did not fire. The situation was silly. There was I with a powerful rifle, within five feet of my quarry, completely and utterly unable to do a thing about it.

Finally I withdrew, cut back into the bush and tried to work round the other side of the boar in the hope of getting a sight on him. But, whatever happened, I did not. I left the scene and, as far as I could judge, the beast was still there, rooting, grunting and snuffling.

With wild cattle the case was a bit different; the only thing wrong about their pursuit was they were never plentiful enough to make the game worth the daylight.

So, for both types of game, dogs were the answer, especially in locating them. Dealing with the pig requires a team of trained dogs. In that camp we had four cross-bred cattle dogs, a bitch and her three sons plus a large bull-mastiff-greyhound with the rather unimaginative name of Bully. As you will see, it should have been Don Castro.

Bully was a master of arts in pig hunting. He would hang round our heels and leave the herd work of "finding" to his under-yappers. As soon as they gave tongue, Bully would stroll down in the direction of the circus and watch proceedings rather like a referee watching a scrummage. Unless it was a tusker that was bailed, this dog hardly deigned to join the show at all. But, if a boar was the centre of resistance, he went in with evident relish, using a method of his own to get the ball out of the scrum, so to speak.

I should have explained that Bully's head and fore parts were bull-mastiff, but his hinder parts were very greyhound. In the technique that he had developed it was the bull end which mattered. Sooner or later the milling dogs would provoke the boar and he would charge one in the hope of getting his tusks to work. Bully would wait for such a moment, and before the charge was completed, he would sail in behind the boar and grab him by that large protuberance that gives the boar his boarhood, and hang on in true tradition of the bull-dog breed: "What I have I hold."

I remember on one occasion in swampy ground when our artful dog had a full mouthful, and the boar was roaring with pain and rage. All the boar could think of was to sit down on Bully's head. Down in the swampy soil went the dog's head until it disappeared under the boar's stern. The greyhound end with its long tail, thrashed helplessly, but still he held on. I was afraid the dog would be smothered, and perhaps he would have been, had my pistol not ended the contest with Bully still hanging on.

Before the old master reached the age of retirement, he was the bearer of many scars from early battles, and one fearful burn mark from when he was caught in a bush-burning fire. It took us a long time to nurse the old fellow back to health after this accident, and he was never able to use his scientific knowledge of ballistics again.

Hunters often returned to the cities from the King Country with legendary tales of great boars. The story of a young friend of mine was about a boar to outdo all boars for ferocity, cunning, tusk, and size. He had himself, so he said, met this animal in a tight corner, and was a very lucky hunter, indeed, to have survived the ordeal.

It seems that this boar became tired of people stalking him and bouncing bullets off his hide. So, whenever he saw a man with a gun he did not wait to be shot but started out to stalk the hunter.

In this way he became something of a legend and was dubbed "The Old Man of Ohura".

From what I remember of Clem's story of his adventure, it seems that he met this terrifying beast on a narrow track and got such a shock that as he rushed to the nearest tree he could hear it snorting and crashing after him. He just made the tree and, dropping his rifle, scrambled up just escaping certain death.

Having plenty of time on his hands, the Old Man of Ohura stopped under the tree and started to take it out of the rifle by stamping all over it. He then decided to dig it in, and to pretty good effect too. Rooting a deepish hole near the butt he then got to the muzzle and started to push the weapon into the trench. Unfortunately for himself, in the process he must have disturbed the trigger, for the gun "suddenly exploded" as the newspapers say, at the very moment the Old Man of Ohura's mouth was wide open; the bullet entered his mouth and killed him stone dead.

A tale is often good for a few tellings. Possibly our young enthusiast used to forget to whom he had related his thrilling experience before. However he was cured of this fault, if fault it was, at a very gay party in mixed company when one of his bibulous pals called out from the far end of the room:

"I say, Clem, old boy. Do tell them that great yarn of yours on how you shot The Old Whore of Manuwera."

10. Trophy Tusks

While many New Zealand hunters go after the porker mainly for meat, they are always on the lookout for a good trophy. There is keen competition in all branches of the New Zealand Deerstalkers Association for the prize boar's head and tusks.

Norman Douglas has established a system for recording the trophy value of boars' tusks, and as far as I know, it has been generally accepted by the association's branches.

Only four measurements are considered:
1. Length of extracted tusk measured under outer curve.
2. Girth at the base of tusk.
3. Girth at the base of grinding.
4. Length of grinding surface itself.

In all four measurements the score is decided on the shorter measurements of the two tusks, doubled.

Grinding: When normally ground, the tusk is ground to sharpness on two of its three corners at the tip. This is brought about by the lower tusk being placed ahead of the corresponding tusk when the mouth is closed. Owing to the circular growth-pattern of the lower tusk, contact with and rubbing occurs on the front face of the tusk above. This upper tusk is called a "grinder", and acts as a lap. In this way the tusks are sharpened, and at the same time prevented from growing too long for use as successful fighting weapons. (*The Douglas Score*, pp. 47–48.)

Mr Robert George Hill, who was a wonderful stalker of boars and stag and was still actively hunting at sixty-five, when we had our last chat, had a collection of thirty or more sets of tusks photographed for the *Fishing & Shooting Gazette*

(August 1950). These were all trophy quality tusks. Though he did not supply us with figures he told us that he once had a single tusk of 26½ inches. This he sent to the Wembley Exhibition of 1924. It was displayed with the collection of New Zealand deer heads in the Dominions' Court from where it was stolen. Under the Douglas system this tusk could not qualify for a prize as it was only half a pair. Anyway there was no official recognition of boars' tusks as sporting trophies at that time; they were merely collected by sportsmen as personal trophies.

No outstanding collectors' tusks ever came my way. All I can claim is an odd pair that would have encircled a small dinner plate. I never measured them accurately as I'm not fond of looking at Sus cookii except over the sights of a gun.

The desire to add a New Zealand trophy to his collection caused an English sportsman to call at the Wanganui office of the manager of Murray Roberts Ltd. It appears he had some knowledge of boar hunting in India where the animal is taken with a spear from the back of a galloping horse. The sport was pursued under code rules and must have held considerable excitement and some risk.

"Ay have been informed," he said, "that your wild boars are *huge*. *Terrific* things armed with vicious tusks. Could you kindly put me in touch with this kaynd of hunting, sir? Ay am quait willing to pay, you know."

The manager put through a telephone call to an up-river development block.

"You will be very welcome up there," he told the sportsman.

And it was so. He was given a clean and comfortable whare that was set apart on a grassy open area. Plenty of advice was given about where he could look for his game. But sheep stations are busy places, so the visitor was left free to look after himself. In high gear and adequately armed he was out on the hills early next morning. He returned late in the evening without having seen hair or hide of any kind of pig.

For several days more his attempts to come to terms with a huge boar were unavailing and he registered a mild protest. "Ay say . . . Ay have come all these blooda males heah to New Zealand. Ay 've spent day after day climbing all over your station without even seeing a boah. Where are these blooda boahs?"

The thought of giving up had not occurred to him.

"Try one more day," he was told. "Something is sure to turn up."

After the visitor had gone off next morning, Kelly Cunningham, a tough and hardened stockman, whistled up his dogs and with a few grain sacks and some rope, set off for a place he knew.

When he returned his men noticed him down at the sportsman's whare. The dogs were with him.

It was nearly sundown when a weary hunter returned to the whare. He might have wondered why half a dozen of the station dogs were running round in some excitement. He had no way of knowing that the station's staff were in hiding close by.

What he did was to open the door and step inside. As he did so all the dogs dived in past him.

What happened in the next few minutes can only be imagined but the tumult that arose from the six dogs assailing a boar under the hunter's bunk was something that was afterwards remembered with awe. Added to the uproar was a cultured voice using words the toughest man envied.

At the moment of his own choosing, Kelly Cunningham hopped in with his sacks and the next thing the men saw was their boss riding the boar with a horny hand gripping each ear of his mount, in a circle outside the whare, and surrounded by the still roaring pack of dogs.

True to the traditions of his race, the visitor took the joke in good part. He shouted generously all round and asked if he could remain on the station as an honorary member of the staff. In time he learned the run of the ropes and did more than his share of the work. Pig hunting, as it was really done in New Zealand, was always his favourite pastime and he had much success.

One of the shepherds was heard to remark: "These English toffs are a special kind of bloke!" No one was heard to disagree.

Although the bush as we know it has largely disappeared there are still places where good dogs are essential in the pursuit of wild pigs. For the most part wild pork is now picked up along the margins of scrubland where pasture grows. Early in the morning and late in the afternoon the pigs come out to forage. Land that has gone back to bracken is favoured. Rootings on green patches can be detected a mile away. As soon as these are located, the climbing can start. With a careful approach and a little bit of luck, a shot can be the reward. Under these conditions the meat should be at its best. A pig that is chased, like any other kind of animal, is more likely to be tough.

A good rifle is the thing for this kind of pig hunting, a telescopic sight being an aid when the light is fading. The short-barrelled or sawnoff blowpipe that can serve well enough in bush where the pig is bailed up by dogs, is useless on bush margins where careful stalking is needed.

The ·22 rim-fire is no good except for brain shots. Not often are conditions right for this kind of fine shooting.

Pigs need at least an 80-grain bullet with a velocity of about 1,500 feet per second. Nothing short of the Winchester ·32-20 (100 grains 1,230 f.p.s.) is really satisfactory.

The ·303 is the usual choice, and though a bit too much for small to medium porkers, is not too much for the boar.

When pistol carrying was ruled out in 1921 it meant that a man broke the law when armed with any weapon with a barrel that was less than 12 inches long "outside the curtilage of his dwelling". To meet this situation and comply with the desires of his customers, a merchant imported a line of small one-hand smooth-bore "guns" with barrels of 12 inches in length. He called the piece a saddle-gun and said it was essential for the use of shepherds in the ranges of the South Island in the destruction of a sheep-killing bird of the parrot kind. No doubt he was quite correct, but someone or other started to complain that these ·410 gauge were not guns at all but were pistols. I was asked for my opinion as to whether the sample sent was a pistol within the meaning of the Act or not.

What I personally thought about this business does not matter. What I did, was to take the thing to the Hutt Railways workshops to get the barrel measured.

There my friend Gordon Haslow swung the barrel between the jaws of an enormous micrometer. The result was, at room temperature, then about 60° F, that the barrel measured 12·006 inches. When the temperature fell to around 45° F, the barrel shortened itself. So, on a warm day it was a shotgun; on a cold one it was a pistol! Well, how silly can we get?

My reply did not include the information that the "saddle-gun" was capable of accommodating a "gamegetter" ball cartridge, but it will.

11. Bush Whirligigs

I have often wondered if people become bushed, not because they do not know the way out, but because they are cocksure that they do! I had an astonishing instance of this in 1908 when four of us were pig hunting for camp meat.

We were mates on a 550-acre bushfelling job on high country between Ohakune and Raetihi, rather north of the present highway between the Mangawhero and the Mangahowhiu Rivers. Our plateau would be about 2,000 feet above sea-level, and some of the ridges and hills rose 1,000 feet higher. The country was heavily forested with abundant undergrowth in which wineberry, konini, matipo, and five-finger were plentifully laced with lawyer vines and supplejacks. The forest was thick with medium-sized trees, mostly bastard birch (tawhera) and tawa. The big trees were rimu, matai, white pine (kahikatea), miro, and totara. Many of these could show trunks of sixty feet and more. It was therefore a glorious place for a bushlover. To complete the picture of the scene of my story it should be added that there were four main spurs that ran at right angles to the main one, upon which we were camped, with steep sided gorges, down every one of which ran ice-cold streams of water that seeped out of the papa country. Some papa sides were naked through slips, and some other places were deeply scored with narrow fissures which could be a few feet across and sixty feet deep. It was, therefore, no place with which to take liberties nor to attempt to traverse after dark.

After we had killed our second pig, a fat half-grown sow, it was time to return to camp. We were jubilant at having such a good supply of meat of the best sort. With some parts salted and packed in a wine cask we would have enough meat for a couple of weeks.

I regret to record that it was the only New Zealander of the party who was the chief actor in this rather terrifying experience. Perhaps as the rest of us were "foreigners" Paddy felt that he was the natural leader. Springing to his feet, he said: "Come on fellers or we'll never get out before dark." Off he struck down the ridge, followed unquestioning by Joe the Tasmanian. The man from Kent, John stood waiting for me. This was the usual pattern: Paddy and Joe versus John and me.

I was moved to call out, "Paddy, you're going to Wanganui that way."

"Don't be silly. Come on, I say, or we'll be caught in the dark."

"But Paddy, we should go uphill." There was no answer as the pair disappeared. John looked scared.

"But what if they get lost?"

"No 'if' about it, John. They'll be lost all right."

John started to yell, "I say, you fellows. I say . . ." and then, "Oh, those silly perishers."

We shouldered our pork and struck straight up the ridge. The least observant should have know our camp was on top of the plateau. Damn Paddy and the silly ass who always swallowed his hero's yarns. I was worried, but I needn't have been.

A long drawn "cooee" came from deep in the bush below. We answered at once and waited. The Tasmanian kept up his "cooee, cooee", and we too kept calling back. It dawned on us that Joe was alone. His answering calls were coming first from one side of the ridge then from the other, and it was plain he wasn't travelling on the top of the ridge as an experienced bushman should.

The bush was getting darker and the voice was still some way below us. I thought of going down the ridge to meet

Joe, but John cried: "Don't leave me; for God's sake, don't leave me."

Then there was movement just below and out burst a figure, not Joe's, but that of the redoubtable Paddy himself. And what a Paddy! His face was streaming with blood from being wiped with the trailers of lawyer vine with their cruel rosebush claws. He had thrown away his beautiful pig. His thin, long sandy hair was plastered down his face with sweat and blood. He still gripped his rifle and I was a bit scared at the mad look in his eyes.

Tact was called for. "Oh, hello, Paddy," I said, "I'm glad you came back. Where did you leave Joe?"

"Comin', I suppose. Bloody fool splittin' up. If you won't let me guide you, we'll camp in the bush. Mus' stick together. *I'll never take out a party of mugs shooting in the bush again!*"

Still far below we could hear Joe yelling out. We answered each yell, but had to wait; it looked as though we should have to camp, as Paddy said.

At last the little Tasmanian struggled up through the bush to us. He seemed little the worse for wear, except that he had lost his hat.

"Why didn't you wait for me, you Irish baster'?" he snarled at Paddy.

I expected trouble, but Paddy had no word. He was trying to fill his pipe and it was almost funny to watch him. His hands shook so badly that he spilled the fillings and the pipe was still empty when a shaky match was held near it.

I thought the least said the better.

True to the traditions of the bulldog breed the man from Kent had hardly spoken, but stood watching our show wide-eyed and pale about the gills. He followed me as I moved up the ridge. Paddy, still cursing and swearing, came next. A chain or so behind staggered, rather than walked, the empty-handed Tasmanian.

I saw something ahead. It was reddish brown. I stopped.

"Paddy," I commanded, "come here." He came up to me. "See that brown thing there?"

"Yes."

"What do you think it is?"

"The portico of the bloody Grand Hotel, I suppose."

"Paddy! That is a dead matipo on the edge of the burn. You're out of the bush and within half a mile of camp."

Paddy and the others rushed past me yelling with joy. When I reached the scorched matipo bush my three mates were going hell for leather along the pack-horse track for camp.

I wasn't able to travel quite so fast, not with a sixty-pound porker on my back.

12. Slightly Technical

War, more than anything else, has been the reason for Man's search for some way of hitting a mark at a distance. His first discovery was that he could hurl a stone; his next that a round stone could be thrown better than a shapeless jagged one. And the day he discovered the virtue of heaviness in relation to size the science of ballistics was born.

As the best warriors of those far-off days were doubtless also the best hunters—and conversely this is still true—a tribe's success depended upon its skill with its arms and its stones. But all men were limited to about the same range at which their game or enemy could be dealt with. A major breakthrough extended this limit with the discovery of the sling.

The earliest record of the sling that I have is to be seen in the wonderful story of David in the First Book of Samuel where he deals with the uncircumcised champion of the Philistines, Goliath of Gath, who defied the armies of God. To those who know the story it is one of the most inspiring examples of courage and faith. Here was a stripling youth who discarded his heavy armour and stood forward to fight this mighty warrior who was clad in the full armour of invincible power; a terror alike to both armies. There he stood, the personification of death and destruction, threatening and scorning the puny David.

But David held in his hand a weapon that was based upon a simple principle of ballistics, the sling, an instrument that could throw a missile with terrific force. Now David knew all this, but he also knew, as every hunter knows, that force is not enough; there must be accuracy as well. Young though he was, he'd had experience with the sling; as a shepherd he had to protect his sheep against marauding beasts and he had felled lions and bears in his day. Goliath could not have known this or he would have taken the shepherd's challenge more seriously.

David had been observed by his people to "gather five smooth stones from the brook", and with his sling in his hand "David took a stone and slung it, and it struck the Philistine on the forehead; the stone sank into his forehead and he fell on his face to the ground."

This is the only record I have of the sling being used as an "engine" of war; and the only one of its use in sport is one of my own. I had one made for me as a toy, and a crude affair it was. The tongue of a blucher boot was cut roughly oval and a bootlace fastened through a hole at each end. My favourite missile was a marble. I could hurl these so far that they were rarely recovered. My standard of accuracy could have been the lowest on record. The family had a large illustrated dictionary and this showed the sling with a cup-shaped holder. Nothing would satisfy me, after that, until I got a cup-shaped holder on my sling. A butcher was persuaded to give me the pouch off the skin of a yearling bull he had killed. By stretching the lower end of this over a cricket ball and lashing it there, it soon dried and hardened into a most satisfying cup. Well, at least, I had a proper sling, though it was not as sweet as violets.

I started an ammunition factory. Cadging pugged clay from Mr Greenwell, the brickmaker, I rolled this into balls and, after they had dried out enough, burnt them in an open fire. I did a lot of practice with these red marbles—they were the size of golf balls and I could recover quite a few of them. I do not know how long my factory lasted, but the last visit I paid to Mr Greenwell is still remembered. Quite rudely, I thought, he almost threw a double-handful of pug at me and snapped, "Take that and don't come for any more." I left the pug where it fell and walked home, crushed and miserable.

The only record of success was when I hit a kookaburra with a bricky on the side of his large intelligent head. Jacky, the kookaburra, was the last thing on the farm that I wished to harm. Remorsefully I ran forward and picked the poor fellow up. His beak was open and for some reason I stuck a finger between the mandibles. They closed on my small finger with such terrifying force that I thought he would shear it right off. But he let me go and I did not need any help to do the same for him.

My next ballistics experiments were with a shanghai with which I raised various samples of hell. My ammunition factory for this weapon did not measure up to the high standard of the one I had organised for my sling brickies. The lead lining from a tea-chest, melted down and poured on to a chopping block, where it soon hardened into a ½-inch sheet, was chopped into cubes. These cubes were superior missiles to my marbles. My chief worry was the supply of lead, so anything in the shape of a lead-head roofing nail, bit of solder or lead pipe that appeared to be surplus to farm requirements went into my ammunition works.

An explosion which threw boiling lead particles all over the shed without hitting my face brought my ballistics research to an end. I wasn't worried much over the loss of my ammunition works for the shanghai, as I became possessed of a real revolver shortly afterwards.

Dionysius of Syracuse is supposed to have invented the catapult in 399 B.C. His must have been a beauty, as it took several men with ropes and levers to cock it. He used it to hurl heavy darts and round stones which must have raised the eyebrows of the Carthaginians. The interesting thing about it was the use of a trigger to release the arm with its cup-like "hand" holding the missile.

Dionysius made no race of his war and was, by his

invention, lifted to the highest position in Greece and became the dictator of his time.

It is also interesting to consider that the Italians, after acknowledging Dionysius as boss, copied his idea and made an engine somewhat better than his to which they gave the name "Ballista".

It is from this word that our own name for the science of ballistics comes. The invention of the ballista clearly reflects man's desire and search for some form of energy greater than that of the muscular power of a single combatant. So this invention of the Greek, which stored up the energy of a bow of such power that it required the strength of many strong soldiers to "cock" it, was as revolutionary in that day as the first British tank was in World War 1.

Sir Edward Poynter, R.A., who painted the ballista in action, must have done much research into its history before making his enormous canvas. He shows the arm being cocked by a crew of soldiery who appear to be hauling the throwing arm, or hammer, with all their strength. The artist depicts, not a ball being hurled, but a large javelin "laid" on aim by a soldier. The besiegers appear to have a whole line of these engines which suggest the origin of the battery.

These cumbersome engines were in use for centuries, mostly for the job of breaching walls of besieged cities. As the ancient gunner had no way of making round iron balls, he used stones, not necessarily round ones.

Although gunpowder was discovered or developed in the thirteenth century its use as an artillery propellant is not recorded until the Germans used it in or about A.D. 1320. Even then, the metallic missile was used very reluctantly. The early gun used stone balls, the cutting, shaping or finishing of which was done by artists and employed for the purpose.

In A.D. 1745 the English Army seized "Mons Meg", the largest of its kind, from the Scots and took it to London. History records that Sir Walter Scott urged its return to

Edinburgh Castle and, despite objections by the Duke of Wellington, it was finally brought back to its present site on the ramparts of Edinburgh Castle.

In 1964 an article appeared in the *Scottish Field* which carried a photograph of "Mons Meg" with several of her cannonballs in place.

I wrote to the editor about the article which was written by Donald Mackenzie, asking what the balls were made of. I received the following reply:

> Thank you for your letter, from which I am delighted to learn that the article by Donald Mackenzie appealed to you. For your information the balls fired by Mons Meg are of stone.
>
> A. E. Comyn Webster,
> Editor.

Whether these were of stone because iron ones were not procurable or because they were more economical, ye ken, is anybody's guess.

Two enormous strides forward in ballistic efficiency were made when gunnery experts decided to abandon the round ball involving the use of heavy guns which were almost useless on a battlefield.

What the gunner was looking for was a gun that would fire a heavy projectile from a smaller barrelled gun that could be moved from place to place. Therefore the cylindrical projectile was the only answer, and it was the first of the two enormous strides.

Having tried long cylindrical projectiles, it did not take the gunner long to realise that this type of projectile was accompanied by a serious falling off in accuracy. Some observant worker then discovered that projectiles were subject to a kind of solar system of their own and revolved in flight. Then it was realised that these cylindrical objects turned in flight on their short axis, or end over end, which made accurate shooting impossible. To counteract this behaviour, it was important that, if a projectile must spin, it should be compelled to spin on its long axis. This forced the development of, perhaps, the greatest advance in gunnery—rifling.

This is a series of spiral grooves which are cut into the side of the bore, leaving a corresponding number of ridges, called lands, between the grooves. The job of the lands is to cut their depth into the outer wall of the projectile and force it to follow their direction and spiral turns as it moves up the bore. It is this spiral impulse that forces the missile, or bullet, into a rapid spin on its long axis, keeping it sharp end foremost as it literally bores its way through the atmosphere.

The accuracy of the weapon depends very materially upon the precision the gunmaker has put into this job of boring a straight "tunnel" in the barrel and the cutting of the grooves. At first, this work was given to workmen who used hand tools. This must have been a long and tedious business until an inventive genius named Eli Whitney of Westboro, Massachusetts, perfected a precision machine to do the job quickly and cheaply.

In 1854 Sir Joseph Whitworth of Manchester, England, was asked by the Government of his day to make a rifle for military use. He did so; but the weapon was rejected, so he went back to ordnance. His passion for accuracy in measurement gave the gunmaker methods of precision in boring and rifling, and on his engineering genius the great firm of Armstrong-Whitworth was founded.

In spite of these two major steps in the evolution of the rifle—the cylindrical projectile and rifling—the flintlock system of setting fire to the powder in the breech was still used.

At its best the flintlock was crude and unsatisfactory. The very nature of its structure necessitated a large metal projection attached to the weapon, usually on the right-hand side of the lock, which, because it resembled a rooster's head was called a cock. It carried appropriate terms for its parts. The body of the huge hammer curved gracefully like a cock's breast. Its flint was held in the beak, and the screw which moved the upper bill had a round ball with a hole through it so that the user could tighten the cock's grip on the piece of flint. This was called the comb.

Our terms "cocking", "uncocking", "half-cock" and so on, follow those of the flintlock system.

The chop was the face of steel against which the flint chopped with violence when the trigger was pulled. This resulted in a shower of sparks flying downward into the pan which held the priming charge of powder. Being pivoted on a forward axle, this chop was free to move upward and forward. The flint's first contact caused the chop to lift exposing the priming powder to the sparks. When fired, a jet of flame passed down the touch-hole into the main charge. Uncertainty about whether it did or did not fire brought into use the saying: "That was only a flash in the pan."

Always, of course, there was the risk of the priming getting wet and squibbing. Oliver Cromwell knew something of this problem when he adjured: "Trust in God and keep your powder dry."

Years were to pass before a sporting clergyman brought about the next great development. The Rev. Alexander John Forsyth, Minister of the Church of Scotland in a small parish near Aberdeen, devised a means of using fulminates to suit his purpose. Fulminates explode with great violence when struck a sharp blow. They were thought by the chemists who discovered them to be too dangerous for use as a propellant or in industry and were put aside.

As a student of science Forsyth became aware of the nature of these chemicals, and in his duck shooting on the marshes must have dreamed of their use to detonate the charge in his flintlock. The story goes that in his experiments, Forsyth made such good progress that he was the first man to throw away his flint and use fulminate in its place.

Following his lead, others worked on his idea until finally the metal cap and nipple came into general use. Still in use is something of the same kind to prime all cartridges, including those known as rim-fire.

Forsyth's invention was given the name of the percussion system and was so reliable that all flintlock types were abandoned in its favour. Under present-day methods of loading, ignition failures are so rarely due to the cartridge that they are practically non-existent.

The search for a sound breech-loading system occupied gunmakers and inventors for many years, even after the percussion caps were in general use on arms that were loaded from the muzzle or on revolving cylinders like the Colt cap-and-ball of 1835.

An interesting example of the in-between stage of development from muzzle-loading to breech-loading is the Terry carbine.

The famous Major von Tempsky's Rangers used the Terry in the Maori wars in Taranaki. The interesting thing about this carbine was that the breech was operated by a bolt which was turned by a lever. Its action was similar to that of a modern rifle but it was loaded in the following manner: a separate bullet was first pushed into the breech and forced forward far enough to admit the powder charge. This was wrapped in a skin at the factory—thus ensuring a correct charge of powder—and was inserted after the bullet. The bolt was then pushed forward and the lever turned down to lock the bolt in place. A separate percussion cap was then placed on the exterior nipple of the breech. When the cap fired, its explosion drove the flaming gas through the skin holding the charge.

A much superior weapon of the kind was made by Remington Arms in the United States; but this one used a coil of caps held in paper. The coil was contained inside a small box on the side of the action and was fed up, one cap at a time, over the nipple by a chisel-shaped pusher. Each time the hammer was cocked, one cap moved up into position.

It was really the invention of the complete cartridge that forced the development of the breech-loader. They were concomitant. The first cartridges were made of iron and brass with paper body. Then sheet metal was used as a wrapper to hold powder and bullet. Finally shells were made of drawn brass to hold primer, or cap, powder and ball. The modern cartridge was born.

Man's desire to hit his enemy at a distance was fully satisfied. The difficulty remains: how to prevent the said enemy from hitting back.

It must be almost time that Man made up his mind that a good gun should be used only for target shooting and for hunting game in the hills.

13. Hit the Thing!

Bad shooting is due to the shooter and not to his gun or cartridge which generally get the blame.

There are three main factors in shooting:
1. The Aim.
2. The Hold.
3. The Let-off.

Any person with reasonable eyesight can aim a rifle. It is simply a matter of lining-up the foresight in the notch or "V" of the rear-sight and holding these on the mark.

This is the simplest of the big three mentioned above. It should result in a pretty fair shot, providing the sights are correctly adjusted on the rifle as they should be. But there are the other two tyrants of "hold" and "let-off" to be obeyed.

Learning the correct hold needs considerable practice with most beginners, as wrapped up in this job are such factors as nerves, excitement, breathing and often, awkward position.

The steadiest position is the one used by riflemen in competition shooting: prone. This is rarely possible when game hunting. The seated position is more readily taken. A good style is to dig the heels firmly into the ground; open the legs as far as possible; place an elbow on each knee—there is a natural pit for the elbow against the knee-cap—press the elbows firmly outward and hold the butt snugly against the shoulder. When it is convenient to rest the cheek down on the stock, this helps to steady the head.

The third of our rules, the let-off of the trigger, is frequently the cause of failure because the trigger is pulled, whereas it should be squeezed.

The sudden yank of this delicate little lever which releases the firing mechanism will almost certainly upset the aligned barrel at the vital moment, and the shot gets misdirected usually to the right and low.

Some modification of this natural mistake of jerking the trigger can be made by using the second finger instead of the usual forefinger. This arrogant digit gets far too much of its own way. It is the boss and hates being told what to do. Its neighbour is a much milder person and meekly awaits orders. As the shooter is, or should be, the one to give the order to fire the shot, he will find the second finger more obedient to his will.

Among the Trentham shooters for the Queen's Prize it is possible to see quite a few whose "know-all" forefinger is resting on the outside of the guard while the second finger is awaiting its orders on the trigger.

Another point: The second finger is nearer to the centre of the gripping hand and takes the strain of the "grip-off" or squeeze-off of the trigger more naturally.

That which the golfer and the snooker player call the follow-through should never be neglected in rifle work. Every effort should be made to hold the rifle "on" after the squeeze off. It is so easy to relax too soon!

Learners can help themselves to success in the hills by first studying these hints carefully, and then applying them in careful and unconceited practice at a target before they grab a gun and go tearing up a gully over the hill looking for blood.

The best of marksmen will agree that the big three are their problem as much as they ever were, even though the movements become second nature. However, this chapter is not written for the rifle-club man. His game is quite different from that of the man in the hills for whom it is written. He has to kill his animal, not merely knock a chip off the side of it.

Some hunters can kill a lot of animals without knowing a great deal about the science of ballistics. Perhaps this is because they find a number of animals to shoot at and have plenty of cartridges to use.

This chapter is intended to give a junior sportsman a chance to understand the power and accuracy of the modern rifle.

The term "interior ballistics" relates to the series of happenings from when the primer of his cartridge is fired into the powder charge until the bullet, a fraction of time later, leaves the muzzle. "Exterior ballistics" relates to the flight of the bullet from the muzzle to its first point of contact.

The value of a proper "hold" and "squeeze-off" is closely related to interior ballistics, and it would pay a sportsman to understand why, even though the series of happenings are imperceptible as such.

Smokeless powder does not really explode or detonate; it burns. The only detonation is the explosion of the priming mixture in the cap of the cartridge.

In the process of burning, the powder converts its small bulk into a great volume of gas.

As soon as the gas starts to generate pressure, the bullet starts on its way up the barrel, gaining speed as it is driven forward under the rapidly rising pressure until it reaches its highest-ever speed at the muzzle. This is a measurable speed, and is called "muzzle velocity" or initial velocity.

The pressure in the barrel rises to thousands of pounds per square inch, say 4,500 lbs in a ·303 rifle. This is a lot of force to send such a small object weighing only 174 grains on its way through the air, and such force has to be contained within the rifle barrel.

Although it is not perceptible except by the use of instruments this force which sends the bullet up the rifled bore, and the passage of the bullet itself causes the barrel to "whip" up and down like a piece of rope. There is no escape from this barrel whip. All that can be done is to damp down its effect by the use of a properly fitted fore-end or fore-stock of wood grooved correctly to act as a "bed" for the barrel.

HIT THE THING! 93

The sights are adjusted to look after this barrel whip or "jump" and if the ammunition is regular—very little is not—the barrel whip does no harm because it is constant.

Anyone in doubt about the truth of barrel whip can settle the question by taking an ordinary sporting ·22 calibre rifle to a small-bore rifle club and trying it out against the inch-thick barrelled club rifles. He will soon be convinced that his own rifle is outclassed by the heavy barrelled rifles clubmen use.

Having a grasp of what happens in his hunting rifle, the young shot will begin to appreciate the great value of a proper hold. He will also appreciate that consistency in his method of hold and the amount of firmness he uses are of equal importance.

Though the period of time from trigger release to when the bullet leaves the muzzle is calculated in ten-thousandths of a second (and takes roughly two-thousandths), it is long enough for a faulty shot if hold and aim are relaxed too soon. Again, the small-bore rifle club practice will confirm this dictum. At the instant of its release from the barrel the bullet becomes subject to exterior ballistics factors. From that instant its forward impulse is opposed by the air through which it has to make its way, and as it has lost the propelling power of the gases it loses speed and energy.

Energy is calculated in foot pounds and is related to the weight of the bullet and the velocity. It is the energy due to these two factors that does the killing. But the bullet has to do the hitting.

The biggest snag in hunting is bullet-drop. Though it is a constant in physics its relation to the range at which the shot has to be taken is much neglected. This bullet-fall is exactly the same whether the bullet is travelling as if it is dropped from the fingers or topples off the end of the barrel.

The value of its forward speed is that it travels quite a distance during a fraction of a second of time. This speed is called velocity. Therefore a high-velocity rifle makes the bullet travel, say, 200 yards while a low-velocity rifle takes the same time to send the bullet 100 yards, because the degree or speed of fall is exactly the same in both cases.

"Point-blank range" a term so beloved of newspapers, does not exist in fact. It merely means that the distance between muzzle and mark is so short that the fall of the projectile is imperceptible.

The importance of understanding this matter of bullet drop is related to the hunter's judgement of distance. How poor most men are at this skill is demonstrated during the duck season. The most ignorant gunner ought to know that a shotgun is limited to an effective range of 55 to 60 yards; but any morning in the swamp or on a lake will see cartridges banged off at twice or three times these distances.

It is true that the rifle user is not so limited. His bullet reaches farther out, but as it is dropping all the time, his judgement of the range can give him a kill or a lost trophy.

High velocity damps down the punishment, as it gives the hunter no problem like that of the man armed with a rifle with less velocity than 2,000 feet per second. With the latter the range of 150 to 200 yards is a good long shot. Whereas he who has a rifle such as the ·270 Winchester (130-grain bullet at MV 3140) has a good chance up to 300 or 350 yards; a range long enough for anyone and too long for most of us.

How far is 100 yards? The answer is a surprise. It is much farther than we think it is!

As we walk across a paddock or along a track we pick a mark ahead of us and say: "That's a hundred yards." We then count our ensuing paces. By the time we've reached sixty we are not far from that mark.

Having a special interest in this subject I have done a lot of this sort of thing and became humbled in consequence. But it gained me a certain wisdom in the matter of judging how much to allow for range. I recommend it.

Sights are set so the line of departure of the bullet is above the line of sight. For game distances it is perilous to change

HIT THE THING! 95

sight adjustments when hunting. They are nearly always overdone. A deer hunter should have his sights set for 200 yards. Should he judge the distance to be, say, 300 he should aim just a little higher on the animal; not worry about pushing up his sliding bar on the rear sight. If beyond 300, leave the beast alone.

Wind pressure will deflect a bullet alarmingly. This is the rifleman's eternal problem. He knows his range to a T as it is measured from mound to target. He knows his elevation for his rifle at each and every distance. But he does not know so exactly what the wind pressure will be *on the instant of firing*. All he can do is to read the flags which stretch the length of the rifle range. Even with all these aids, he can miss at 800 or 900 yards, not through elevation troubles, though these happen at times, but through the bullet being blown to one side of his ten-foot wide target.

The hunter can only judge the force of the wind by such things as trees and bushes or even snowgrass and tussock. Therefore long-range shots at game in windy conditions are a wild gamble, and ought to be avoided.

So far we have been dealing only with open-sighted rifles. Where aperture sights are possible they are of assistance in defining the mark. Nearly all of these aperture or peep sights are fitted with screw clicking adjustments which are grand for getting the sights set correctly at a target *before we leave home*. They should be left strictly alone in the hills.

Telescopic sights are something for the expert who is already far outside the orbit of these bits of advice from me. Where they can be used, of course, there is nothing half so good, but under adverse conditions they can bring troubles galore. I use them whenever possible. They are marvellous, they are beautiful and they are very easily damaged.

Armed with the realisation that the essentials outlined must be observed, any man can be successful provided the animals he wants to get are in the hills and that he had the wind and the muscle to scramble over them.

Ten cartridges fired in conscientious practice to every one fired at game makes a good start for any hunter. If he joins a rifle club he will rub shoulders with real marksmen and learn much wisdom.

If, on the other hand, he has not given attention to these matters, and "Just goes out for a shot" he might decide to miss this chapter; and keep on missing.

Boyds Rock stands above beech forest and snowgrass country in the mountains east of the Tongariro National Park. In the foreground is the Auster aircraft in which the author flew out of the mountains.

(Photo author)

Les Mark, of Taumarunui, with his pet stag and its family on his farm.

(Photo *N.Z. Herald*)

14. *This Queer Madness*

Peter Scott, speaking from London many years ago, used the term "this queer madness" to describe his search for migrating geese. In those days Scott was hunting the bird with a gun. His experiences and his sufferings gradually built up his profound respect for his beautiful quarry and finally led him to devote his life to its study and protection.

As far as I and all other duckshooters are concerned the "queer madness" recurs annually and lasts from mid-April to the end of the shooting season—and a bit longer. The "malady" sets every duckshooter an urgent problem—the finding of a place to shoot.

To the gunner of fifty years ago, great areas of publicly owned swampland, lagoons, lakes and lengths of river bank were open. Even then there was often a wild scramble for select spots. It was every man for himself and no sympathy for the loser. These "open" lands are now so drastically reduced by modern drainage development that the problem is even more serious. Land hunger has lifted prices to a level where costly drainage and development schemes have been undertaken by the Government and farms now flourish where once only the pukeko and bittern had their home. Farmers who bought these marginal farms were obliged to take advantage of the value of the duckshooting stands, either keeping them for themselves or friends or trading them one way or another. The general effect was the same; they were lost to the public. Side by side with the shrinkage of swamp areas came the big rise in the number of competitions. There are today about 10,000 of us in the Auckland district alone.

The wild scramble first came under my notice in the Waikato district. Here were hundreds of acres of Mad Hatter's gardens of flax, niggerhead, fern, cuttygrass, willow, raupo reeds and giant fescue. I was told that they were railways reserve and open to anyone who could get there and claim a place not already staked. Why a railways concern should have any interest in such a place puzzled me. I was not to know that the coal beds beneath them would feed the huge Meremere electric power house at Mercer.

In my new appointment with an Auckland sporting goods business I met many gameshooters who called for licences, service and supplies of ammunition and gear. So it was natural that I soon heard of wonderful places to shoot. Names new to me became familiar: Rangiriri, Piako, Waikato Heads, Matata, Wairoa; but somehow it was the attractive cadence of Whangamarino that caught my imagination.

Whangamarino! It became a talisman, a name to play with, not unlike the words You Yangs did in my boyhood. The Whangamarino-Kopuku region with its hundreds of acres of shallow wetlands was to become for me a school for this kind of wildfowling. From the beginning I was to find the place as fascinating as it was to be, at times, frightening.

As the opening day of 1923 drew near my chances of claiming a stand in the swamp faded. One day into the showroom walked a farmer from Otahuhu who has become a legend.

"Mr Kelly?"

"Yes."

"My name is Shepherd. A friend said that you know about guns. I want a good one. Not a hundred guineas, you know, but reliable and with a good pattern."

"What do you wish to use it for?"

"Ducks mostly and pheasants."

This was the man who not only introduced me to Whangamarino but was to be my staunch shooting companion on many splendid occasions. Of all the shooting men I have met Ernie is the most devoted to this sport of duckshooting. He is little interested in any other kind of sport. My efforts to get him interested in rifle shooting to which I was devoted, were wasted. Gun-club shooting at clay birds was quite without appeal for him; but give him the chance to get wet feet on a dark winter's dawn with wild wings whistling overhead and this hard-headed judge of livestock would grow highly excited and feverish. Though we have not shot together for thirty-five years I am glad to record that Ernie can still enjoy his favourite pastime and still shoots with the solid hammerless non-ejector that I fitted him for and patterned for him.

Every subsequent season till I left Auckland in 1935, Ernie fixed up a place for me to shoot. We both liked to shoot alone, and on no occasion did we work together except in upland searching for ground game.

Transport was often a problem. Usually I went by train to Mercer where Ernie picked me up. On one occasion he was unable to do so, as he had his "new" launch tied up at the Kopuku Landing. I was advised to travel by bus which would drop me at a point on the main road within walking distance of the landing.

That night the Auckland province turned on one of its notorious rainstorms. As we drew near to my debussing point I thought with some uneasiness of my projected march, loaded with gun, ammunition and other essentials. A pretty fair load. Moving forward I had a lowvoiced word to the driver: "Three half-crowns."

"I'll do what I can, sir."

At the turn-off he stopped.

"Ladies and gentlemen," he said, "have you any objection if I take this passenger down to the landing?"

There was a silence which did not cheer me.

"He's a duckshooter and has a launch waiting for him. He's got a fair load of gear and doesn't really know the way."

The reply was immediate and made music for me above the roar of the downpour. As I swarmed out at the landing almost into the arms of a member of the crew, and murmuring my thanks to everyone, several male voices called: "And good luck to you, mate!" There are times like this when the courtesy of the average New Zealander warms the heart.

The deluge continued for hours and the level of the swamp rose and rose. Warm and dry in the four-man cabin, it was lucky we had made no attempt to camp on the bank. About midnight the rain stopped as suddenly as it had started. My companions were jubilant at the rain, knowing that the rising of the water meant the ducks would spread over the whole swamp and everyone would get a fair chance of some shooting.

In the predawn darkness Ernie piloted me to my *maimai*. It was just big enough for my little flattie. The higher water lifted me above the level of the walls of the *maimai*—I was head and shoulder above them! This would never do when full light came or I would be spotted at once and avoided. I was grateful again to my friend who had tossed a fruit-case into the boat as a seat, and I was able to sit down instead of stoop. There was a fairly thick drizzle and not a breath of the wind we had hoped for.

All about the swamp men were moving, rowlocks creaked, voices, sometimes cursing, were heard. Dogs barked on the marginal dairy farms; a train roared across a bridge sounding much closer than it was. My torch showed the legal time of shooting (6.30) was drawing near. No duck wings were heard! This was a feverish moment. There is no way of predicting what the ducks will do. They come or they don't come.

A gun crashed. The usual divine lunatic had beaten the clock. The pukekos, until then apparently only chatting to one another, broke into wild screaming; a flight of black swans flew overhead high out of range. Of the exciting whistling of duck wings there was still no sound.

All around the guns were soon banging in a rising volume. Ernie was nearest to me and his new gun had had its say. I was not sure where the other two members, Alf Burnand and Bill Montgomery, were. I felt I was the only man on the scene with clean barrels. Just as I was beginning to suspect my place was dud, I was caught off my guard when half a dozen black forms flew over me within range and were gone. My barrels were still clean.

"Come on, Greg. Get your gun going!" It was Ernie's voice. Hell. Nothing seemed right. My little craft was so narrow and tippy that I just *had* to lash it to a side stake. Should have done this before. The drizzle had petered out and the water mists were dissolving by this time and I discerned the black masses of swamp scrub looming around me. My decoys looked a bit stupid; one on its side and another upside down. Suddenly big flights poured in and over the whole area. Here is the moment of The Day, that glorious first hour of madness. Later I counted seven ducks down and knew I had killed others which I hoped to retrieve before the hawks found them. It was time to pick up. One duck was bobbing about a bit. I knew the answer. An eel was breakfasting at my expense. I grabbed the duck, but my unwanted rival disputed possession. My flattie tipped dangerously as I leaned over the side to chop him in two with my trailmaker.

The skies were now clear and the main flight was over. Boats were busy everywhere; gundogs were here and there, working under orders and grabbing any duck they saw, no matter who shot it, while high in the blue sky long strings of ducks headed for other waters, possibly the Pacific Ocean.

15. "Poor Old Swan!"

The black swan (*Chenopis atrata*) was introduced to Nelson from Western Australia, where it is the State emblem, about one hundred years ago.

Finding the lakes and swamps of New Zealand to its liking, this large and handsome bird prospered and multiplied to such an extent that it has spread over all the lake country and is present in thousands in Canterbury, Wairarapa, Waikato and Hawkes Bay. It is not plentiful in the central districts of the North Island. At Taupo it is rarely seen except in some of the bays at the southern end of the lake. On Rotoaira, which is a game refuge, I have not seen one in my last dozen visits.

I met the black swan about 1924 in the Whangamarino swamps near Mercer when Ernie Shepherd asked me to join him in the opening of the game season. Later, we were to share some wonderful sport, and, incidentally, some pretty tough experiences. One trip took us up to the Kaipara district to a cattle station known as Ohakakura where Ernie went to purchase cattle, as this was his business.

Mr Pierce, the manager, told us that there had been a liberation of turkeys at one time, and that the birds were quite wild. He invited us to "take a shot" at them if we got a chance. This we did, bagging five. Four of these were fine birds and in good condition, the other was rather on the thin side.

Our visit there was very pleasant. We shot several pheasants and it looked as though we were in for a fine holiday, but Mr Shepherd caused it to be cut short by buying all the cattle available in one fell swoop.

Early next morning, our last day, Ernie said to me: "Come and we'll try to get some ducks and swans. I know where to go."

Thick cover grew to the edge of a swamp, so we had no trouble in sneaking close to the water, but there was a strip of twenty yards over which we would have to sprint in order to get close enough to the surprised birds before they could fly out of range. It was exciting while it lasted. I remember the ducks got away quickly and the swans less so. Two swans flew past me to the left—I was the left-hand gun—and both came down with a crash. I found afterwards that I had loaded with pheasant load (No. 6 shot) by mistake. For swan one needs heavy shot, No 3 or 4 at least, yet these two huge birds had crumpled with No 6 as, luckily, I had overdone the leading and their heads and long necks had caught the dense pattern. I wonder how much we really know about the killing ability of shot?

Shepherd got a pheasant with a beautiful shot on the way back to the homestead.

When we came to pack up it was to find that the four good turkeys had been stolen and the thin one left! We left it too.

Always, or nearly always, Ernie and I got a few swans during the following trips we had together to the Whangamarino and Kopuku swamps. Always, of course, the duck took precedence and the swan was incidental, but welcome.

I missed my old pal and his son Claude when, in 1935, I moved to Wellington. In the job I had taken, it was not possible to spare the time to travel back to Waikato, as the Supreme Court May Sessions open on the first Tuesday in the month. It was rare (I cannot remember one occasion) that someone or other had not been called upon to answer the charge of pulling an unlawful trigger, and I had to be there to tell the Court what that truthful witness, the gun, had told me. So my duckshooting had to be confined to Saturday and Sunday somewhere close to Wellington.

Being born under a lucky star as a duckshooter, I was able

to get in some splendid shoots at Lake Hatuma with Ted Haldane of Waipukurau who, when he heard of the fix I was in, asked me to shoot with him and his father. I had known Ted for a long time. We had shot in the National Rifle Championships for years; he for Waipukurau and I for Auckland City.

E. T. Haldane was an expert duckshooter as well as a first-class rifleman. Like his father he was a thorough gentleman in every way and a most amusing mate in a *maimai*, with the knack of mimicking imaginary remarks by other shooters around the lake:

"That's Haldane over there. Always gets the best place on the lake. Calls ducks for miles. No show being near him with that damn caller of his."

"Who's the long bloke with him?"

"Aw, I dunno, some stranger, they say, from Auckland."

"Wonder why the old man don't shoot with him instead."

"No. Old Bob likes to be alone. He's next, behind the raupo."

"They always do well. The old man owns the farm. So suppose it's fair enough."

"Good shot, old Ted Haldane. See that, a beauty!"

"Those buggers must be gettin' near the limit," and so on.

I soon noticed that Ted did not shoot at swans. Any that came my way, if my shot was good enough, he would go for in the boat and bring in. As eels were bad and would soon take or spoil anything left on the water, this was necessary, but every time Ted brought back my big bird he would say quite sadly:

"Poor old swan."

While "good old Greg" might be a remark following a shot at duck, my swan fell in absolute silence, or nothing more than: "Poor old swan."

This evident fondness for the swan in a man like Haldane who loved his duckshooting so much, puzzled me. Nothing else got this sort of sympathy. He dropped a "pook" (pukeko) with satisfaction: "Those devils pulled Dad's wheat stack to pieces one year," he said. "Picked out a straw at a time to get the grain off the tops."

Finally the "poor old swan" song caught up with me. I got less and less pleasure out of killing them until now I am inclined to let them go, unless the shooting is otherwise too flat to be amusing.

The last afternoon I shot at Ted's was from a friend's house —like *maimai* on the southern end of the lake. From there a wonderful view can be had of the whole of the water, and much of the beautiful Hawkes Bay country beyond it.

Over the two-mile stretch of the lake hundreds of swans had gathered. Some apparently asleep, with their heads lying back on or under their wings, floated like large decoys. Others moved about restlessly. Further skeins came in from over the hills and far-away, their great wings flashing white along the near side of their perfect "V" formation. No doubt an old and wary cob in the lead would set his wings first and all the others did the same. Each lot that came in to the lake followed the leader with the same confidence and precision, and all added to the enormous rafts already on the lake, safe from the dangerous margins where eager guns were watching.

I was alone, as Ted had had a golf appointment at 1.30, so saw the last of that wonderful day.

As the sun bent down to the green hills on my left he threw, as largesse, his changing robes on this lake of a thousand swans. His royal purples damped down to bronzes, his reds to shades of orange and yellow, his silver to newly broken steel. The duckshooter's day was over, and, as the pure air chilled in the fading light, I unloaded my gun, gathered up my gear and the three ducks I had shot after Ted left me. Stepping gingerly into the little green duck-boat I paddled and poled my way back along the darkening tunnel through the bulrushes, and willows to the grassy edge where my pal, back from his golf, met me with the truck. For the three days we had collected thirty-four ducks. I had a few swans and some "pooks".

I distinguished myself next day by leaving for Wellington by train and was miles along the way before I remembered that my "bag" including seventeen ducks was still hanging in Haldane's car shed!

I shall always remember my shoots at Hatuma and those two fine sportsmen Robert Haldane and his son Ted. Both were taken into the Silence long before their allotted span was run.

Perhaps I never really enjoyed shooting the subject of Ted's litany, the poor old swan.

16. Upland Game

Upland game and a gundog are inseparable. And as I refused to keep a dog on a quarter-acre section my chances at the longtails were limited until George Wohlmann offered me a loan of his Mack.

"You'll like this dog, Kelly. He's very biddable." And so he was. I asked George what words of command Mack understood. Mack soon chummed up to me as all gundogs did in those days as my clothes were always permeated with the smell of gunpowder smoke. This is not suprising as I was shooting in sport, target work, experiment or instruction every day of the year. I was grateful for the loan of this fine animal as I had a trip planned for an upland shoot of only one day at Kaikohe in the heart of the pheasant country and had been invited to join a small party. The farm was an abandoned property where secondary growth was spreading to cover vanishing grassland. This is the sort of place pheasants and quail enjoy. There was plenty of cover for them and yet enough open land for foraging. One of the plants favoured by pheasants is inkweed, and this grew in the shallow gullies. There was also redshank to be found in damp patches.

Game was far from plentiful that day, as the season had opened at least a week earlier, but for all that, we got some very fair sport. I had one embarrassing moment when the gun on my right let both barrels go at a cock and missed. The bird flew over and in front of me towards a grove of saplings. I fired and down he came into a mass of tangled vines, where he could have been lost. Mack had him out in no time. He made no mistake and brought him to me with that tail-wagging delight that is so flattering to the gunner.

My day ended with three cocks and a few quail, and Mack seemed quite satisfied with me.

That evening one of the party, the local bank manager, entertained us in his quarters. He had done extremely well in the morning on duck, but was not happy in the afternoon, finding himself flinching.

"Kelly, mine is a new gun but I'll have to get rid of it. It kicks like the devil. Look!" He opened his shirt and his "flinching" was fully explained. His shoulder and upper arm to the biceps was black and blue!

"Could I see your gun, please?" I said.

It was a double-barrelled, hammerless, non-ejector, of quite good quality. I guessed the weight at 7 lbs. A glance at the dismantled barrels showed it was bored to use a $2\frac{1}{2}$-inch cartridge.

"What ammunition do you use?"

"The same as I've always used in my old gun—Noble's Ballistite." A $2\frac{3}{4}$-inch length of shell.

"That is your trouble. The Ballistite is a splendid cartridge, but is too long for these chambers."

"But they go in all right."

This is an old, old story. What my friend had not realised was that the crimp of the cartridge that holds down the overshot wad needs room to unfold and still leave the cone free. The cone is the sloping section which guides the shot into the true tube bore from the larger chamber. To anyone looking at this cone from the breech end, it looks like a step. So, though the longer $2\frac{3}{4}$-inch cartridge "goes in all right" it has no room to unfold the crimp. This means, of course, that the whole violently driven loads of shot and wads are forced through a restricted space. It stands to reason that breech pressures are boosted highly and naturally the recoil is also. The shoulder has to take the resulting heavy kick.

"Well, how is a fellow to know all this unless he's told? The shopkeeper did not tell me. I know nothing about those funny marks on the bottom of the barrels. How is a fellow to know?"

"Drop a sixpence into the chamber, see that it is square across, and measure the distance from it to the breech. If the measurement is only $2\frac{1}{2}$ inches, you use *only* $2\frac{1}{2}$ inch cartridges. Don't forget to take the sixpence out again!"

"Well, I'm blowed," said the banker. I'll never know whether he meant to express surprise at the lesson or resented the suggestion that a good banker would ever leave sixpence in the wrong place. However, we parted very good friends. I was sorry, in a way, he was not my banker.

His problem would not be quite the same today. Ballistite has been abandoned and modified mixtures are now used. For another thing, the old $2\frac{3}{4}$-inch cartridge load can be had today in a shell which can be used in a gun like this. But in the 1930s his cure was to use the lesser load ($2\frac{1}{2}$-inch) or get his gun rechambered to take the longer shell.

He would, with proper ammunition, now find his going a bit better. Always the New Zealander can get 12-gauge ammunition easier than any other gauge, as only 12's are made here. The importing of the other sizes has never been very simple and now is difficult under trade restrictions on overseas funds. Anyhow, the rugged New Zealand sportsman is rarely interested in the fashion of many overseas visitors of using smaller gauge guns for upland shooting. He is quite content to use his 12-gauge for all purposes. For this reason the demand for 16-gauge and 20-gauge guns is small. The advantage of these smaller bores lies with their lighter weight.

My Kaikohe friend had obviously grown weary of carrying a gun weighty enough to absorb the recoil of heavy loads without too much discomfort, and had found his lighter 7-lb much easier to carry. On long rambles over his kind of pheasant country a few ounces of gun weight can be very important.

The ballistic disadvantage of smaller calibres is the fewer pellets of shot to the charge. Supposing the initial velocity is the same—around 1,070 feet per second over the first twenty yards—there are fewer missiles on the way. A 12-gauge cartridge loaded with 1⅛ oz of No 6 shot contains 304 pellets. The 16-gauge has 1 oz (270) and the 20-gauge ¾ oz (208). (Note: There's a tolerance of two pellets up or down.)

The pellets from all three are just as deadly for the bird, but they've got to hit him. This calls for choke-bored barrels and for much more accurate marksmanship.

The overseas visitor might be well advised if he brings his own gun or guns other than 12-gauge, to bring his own ammunition for these odd gauges with him. The same goes for ·410 gauge, (practically useless in New Zealand) used here mostly by orchardists for pest control.

There is another in-between gauge. This is the 28 (2½-inch, $\frac{9}{16}$ oz). Nobody has ever enlightened me why it was ever adopted.

17. "The Mallard has Saved the Grey"

Many shooting men can never resist calling at a gunshop. I am one of these. It was in April 1948 when I called at Arthur McCarthy's in Dunedin. Mac and his manager, Arthur Millar, were sympathetic to my problem, for they know duckshooters well. As their guest I was supplied with a set of decoys, a caller, and "anything else" I might need. Millar rang the secretary of the Acclimatisation Society and this resulted in a "guest" complimentary shooting licence. Hospitality is the keynote of the South.

I made tracks for Omakau in Otago Central where Constable Ward and his son John had fixed up a place for me to shoot. At the local pub I was welcomed and treated like one of the family. On the way out to the selected spot on Stafford Bros. farm I was told that the district was full of ducks. "Farmers grow hundreds of acres of peas here for seed. The ducks know about this; they *like* peas. You can shoot fifteen a day, all mallards if you like, but no more than five greys."

When I saw the chosen spot I was not impressed. The pool was tiny, one of a series of such pools that were dotted along a depressed natural fold in the pastureland. Mine was the biggest of these pools. The only growth apart from grass was tussock which grew along the margin. My friends had built me a hut, as the Southerners call a *maimai* or a hide, by digging a hole in the clay bank and fringing it with three-foot high tussocks, which they had dug out in big clumps—roots, soil, and all. The idea was that the occupant sat down to conceal himself and jumped up to shoot. It looked as though I'd have to hop up pretty quickly to fire.

Ducks, being nocturnal feeders, end their foraging with the approach of daylight and look for a sheltered quiet water for preening, a bit of play and a sleep. This little pond seemed quite inadequate.

That evening I joined a party in the house bar where, naturally, the talk was about duckshooting on this eve of the Glorious First. It came as a distinct shock when one farmer said to me, "Thank God for you duckshooters! If it were not for you fellows we pea farmers would be ruined."

"But," I gasped, "I've never heard of such a thing in the North Island as too many ducks!"

"Well now, look here," he rasped, "if you had put in thirty acres of peas for seed and blasted ducks had gobbled a third of the crop, you'd have a different idea about them."

Next morning the stars seemed to hang along the ridges as I dressed; the curtain by my open window was without movement. It was a hard frost. These conditions were, next to fog, the very worst for wildfowling.

John Ward called for me and ran me out close to my pond. The frost had frozen the grass which crackled under my wading boots as I walked. I found the edges of the pool frozen to three or four feet from the verge. The decoys were soon set out and I planted myself, gun and gear, in the gravelike hole in the clay and pulled the "door" of tussock sods shut. It was intriguing to see the rushes freeze together again in the early daylight. My fingers and toes felt that they were doing exactly the same.

Several times before half-past six I heard wings overhead. The sound was as music, even though the birds all seemed in a hurry to go somewhere else.

Daylight came and I loaded up, keeping in mind the risk of bumping the muzzle against the clay walls, thus "wadding" up the barrels. I had seen quite a few guns blown up through this sort of thing. Nothing happened. A dozen ground-larks were pecking at some kind of food they found on the ice sheet around the verge. A harvester spider climbed slowly up a rush

Canada geese make a fantastic sight as they are driven to banding pens on Lake Ellesmere.
(Photo N.Z. Dept. of Internal Affairs)

Superb stalking country: River and mountain in the Haast region of south Westland.

(Photo David Osmers)

in front of me. Like Robert the Bruce's little cavemate in Ireland, he kept slipping back but "tried and tried again". I wondered what he would do when he reached the top of the rush which stood erect and alone. Finally he made it. As I watched he started stretching his four front legs forward, with the greatest care, along and around the rush. When he was satisfied with this operation, he did the same with his hind legs downwards. I'm certain that if I had not seen the whole movement I should never have spotted him there. He was the colour of the rush, which now looked as though it had a slender two-inch long swelling near the tip. I was never to find out what the little fellow's purpose was for, at that moment, a pair of mallard roared over the pond to swing in a wide circle and fly back over me and the decoys. The faithful Watson spoke to them and they folded and fell, the duck on the grass and the drake on his back among the decoys, his bright orange legs and feet waving slowly.

The hush over the whole place resumed. The larks had vanished and I'd forgotten the harvester spider, which I saw no more. Suddenly ducks came again and again. They were all in small lots and were mostly mallards.

By 7.40 I had killed the limit. My last bird was a grey which fell to the second barrel out on the pasture and had to be chased and shot again.

As I was laying the birds side by side out on the bank, ducks were still flying over and two came and settled. We stared at each other a second or two before they burst into the air and away.

Without a shadow of doubt my success was due to the cunning way in which the Wards had built my hut. They had used only the natural growth, tussock, to disguise the hole in the bank. An incoming mallard would see nothing "new" or strange. The sort of *maimai* we build for grey, of almost anything, will not serve for the mallard. One might be called Simple Simon and the other The Artful Dodger.

As I left Omakau next morning to catch my train for

Oamaru where I had an appointment, I mentioned to one of the chaps my surprise at the larger proportion of mallard to grey.

"Yes," he said, "and a very good thing too. As a matter of fact, we say that the mallard has saved the grey for us!"

18. The Earthquake's Gift

Having been through all kinds of trials on "open" waterways it came as a distinct relief when, through the good offices of Constable Pullinger, I was invited to a secluded property and given the sole privilege of shooting there. It was the first year of my retirement and I was sixty-five. At the end of a sixty mile drive I was taken by the constable to meet my host. We met by the woolshed. Ahead of me I could see some low land that faintly resembled swamp and concluded that was to be the scene of my opening morning. The following conversation left me a most astonished duckshooter and a sorely puzzled one.

"Anyone ever shot here before, Mr Romayne?"

"No. My father would not allow any shooting here and I have not either."

"Why have you made an exception in my case?"

"Well, the constable here says you are stuck for a place to shoot, and that you are a man who shoots with restraint."

"Well," I replied, "I take the limit if I can. I do not shoot at duck on the water, but only in flight."

"Well, those are my reasons," he said.

"Where is the water?"

He pointed up a steep hillside indicating a broken and blackened stump and said it was up there.

I looked for a twinkle in his eye, but he appeared to be quite serious.

"How does water hang on a hillside?"

"You better go up and have a look," he answered a bit sharply; then relented.

"You see, the whole range along the top has been split lengthwise. Probable earthquake many years ago. On this side the subsidence caused a basin to form and in the bottom there is permanent water. It's not very big, but the ducks go there all right."

"Any trees or bushes round the edges?"

"No."

"What grows around it?" I asked incredulously.

"Nothing like trees. Just a few logs have slid down the slopes, otherwise there's only grass."

This was really something new!

"Well," he said as I gaped at the hills around me, "you better go up and look at it. *If* you're interested."

Again there was a slight edge to the voice.

"Thank you, Mr Romayne," I replied, "I shall."

The constable came with me. My heart was not in this business but I just had to be nice about it.

We climbed the steep hill. It seemed to be hundreds of feet up there. At last we reached the rim of a sharply edged basin. I could see that it covered about fifteen acres in all. Masses of earth and rocks were humped in all directions. Huge rata and rimu logs covered the downward slopes. We could see a small pool of muddy water at the bottom perhaps three hundred yards away from where we stood.

"George," I said, "I appreciate what you have done for me but you can see that this place is positively no good for a duck shoot.... Listen! I can hear ducks quacking." At that moment there was a roar of wings as about forty greys took to the air.

We hurried down to the pool. It was quite small, only about seventy yards by fifty. It was, as stated by the owner, destitute of vegetation except pasture grass. A large rock showed above the surface at one end.

Hurriedly we dragged sundry logs and dead fern trunks together to form some kind of a *maimai*, our efforts watched by two white draughthorses, some sheep on the pasture and a few wild goats high on the broken cliff above us.

This is the Hillside Pool. I have shot there every year since that memorable day.

My first morning's shoot gave me a limit bag in about half an hour. My first shot came just before seven o'clock and by about twenty minutes past seven I was within one bird of the limit. My last shot came at a bird that was one of a mob of about a dozen. As it was flying straight away from me I fired at it as it was rising at a vertical angle. I fired only one barrel and was astounded to see two ducks hit the grassy bank and actually bounce backward. I have often thought how thin my excuse for that extra duck would have sounded if a magistrate had to listen to it. As it was, there were more ducks pitching into the pool when I was gathering up my kills and the decoys. It was with high hopes that I returned to the pool next morning only to find that the birds had given the pool a wide berth and my few chances netted me five.

A change came when Mr and Mrs Romayne kindly invited me to stay with them at the homestead. This was a tremendous help saving me, as it did, the early morning drive of sixty miles often through fog. More than this, it gave me the opportunity of getting there a day early, so I could get my *maimai* rebuilt and my decoys ready at the pool the night before the season.

That year also saw a change for me in the placing of the *maimai*. We had chosen the new spot as it was on a sugarloaf of sandstone about half-way along the pool. It was decided to dig a trench into the mound and cover it in the normal manner, but this time a waterproof was arranged with a cow-cover; this, in turn, covered with greenery to disguise it. It was different from the usual in that it was "back on" to the water. It was intended to give the birds a better chance to get a fair start. It meant that when they pitched in, the gunner had to back out of his trench and step round one side or the other. Of course the ducks exploded into the air and the shooting therefore was more difficult and much more exciting. It worked a bit too well, as I found myself missing many left-barrel shots through being too slow off the mark.

This would have been all right, for the extra excitement compensated for the misses, but the birds were fewer that day. Some there were that did not pitch in at all, merely swooping over the water and streaking away without even being seen from the *maimai*. So the following year the roof was pushed off. Once more I could stand up and take my shots as they came—and went—over and out. Two paradise duck got the shock of their lives on this latter occasion. They had no intention of coming in, and were stooging noisily along the far side of the pool at well over 100 feet. Both shots connected and the two big birds hit the grass thud, thud, and only one had to be chased.

That was the last time I climbed up the steep hillsides to the pool on my two feet. I recall that, as I was gasping my way up one of the steepest pinches, and my one good lung was doing its best, I was startled by a great grey shape leaping to life under my feet and vanishing into the darkness ahead. I had seen pig-root several times before, but this was the first boar I had met there. If this beast, a tusker, had charged me, I would have been completely at his mercy. As it was he must have got as big a scare as I did and moved much faster.

As I was leaving the homestead next day for home, my host said: "Kelly. You're getting a bit too old to scramble up those hills. Next year I'll take you up there on the tractor."

Although I thanked him for the offer I thought to myself: "That will be the frosty Friday."

I had been reading in the *Journal of Agriculture* the records of accidents with these machines. At that time a life was being lost about every three weeks. I treated Hector's offer as something of a joke and thought no more about it.

Three hundred and forty-four days later I was to learn that the tractor threat had been nothing of the kind. I was just picking up the last of my gear for the long climb to the pool when I heard the engine of the rubber-wheeled tractor start up with a business-like roar. This was D-Day.

Argument would have been rank ingratitude and, as I knew well enough by now, useless. I lashed my precious gun to the two-bar—well wrapped—hung my knapsack on the back of the seat and perched myself alongside my friend. Tractor seats are rather basin-shaped and intended to accommodate one posterior only. Truly, they will take a big stern but, at the best, do not leave much room for a second one, even a lean one. So all I could do was to grip Hector's far shoulder and perch myself, one buttock in the basin and the other on the rim, and sit more or less side on. My right foot found a resting place on the shaft cover and the left dangled over the side near the left wheel. I don't know where my heart was. From my seat there was no sign of any front wheels though I knew there just had to be. As it happens they are quite small and close together right in the middle. Two headlights projecting outwards from the head of the monster seemed to gleam malevolently as we rolled down the driveway from the house through swirling drifts of fog. I was not quite prepared for the swift right-hand turn of the driveway and was glad of the grip of Hector's shoulder. The nosedive that followed the turn stopped short at a Taranaki gate. We then trundled down a steady slope for a few chains and swung sharply right and jerked to a stop in order to get into lowest gear before plunging madly at a steep trackless face. The machine canted as something turned over in my stomach. I wanted to ask an urgent question but before any word came we left-turned and went straight down as my insides jumped right up. The machine bounced at the bottom, rolled over or through a patch of swampy stuff and roared forward to another Taranaki gate. Once through this we were on a well-defined track still in lowest gear, climbing steadily as the track wandered round the face of a steep hill. A lone conifer caught my eye as I glanced up at the towering crags above.

It looked a strange thing standing there alone and etched against a fragment of faintly paling sky.

Near it was a broken stump with a half-rounded top. "Tombstone" I thought, and quickly looked away.

There had been no conversation so far on the journey. My host was busy with his gears and steering. I remembered the dictum in the Wellington buses: DO NOT CONVERSE WITH THE DRIVER. I no longer thought it an unwarranted interference with the privileges of a passenger. I was still in a beady sweat of nervousness. The track seemed to narrow at this point. I watched the huge wheel under my left foot. It was pretty close to the edge of a two-foot drop. The machine jarred and slipped a bit my way. In horror I saw the edge crumbling under my wheel as the tractor seemed to tilt, but the big tyre rolled onwards and gripped the far side and lifted the machine level once more. I looked at the man behind the wheel. His face was impassive. Then he said: "Do you see that ram there?"

I hadn't noticed anything but that wheel sinking and rising again but looked ahead and saw a sheep moving away in the fog.

"Ye-es. Hector," I stammered.

"Well. I got first and special prize with him at the Waikato Show last year."

"Oh. Good for you."

I was glad when the machine stopped and we offloaded. From there it was only a few hundred yards to the *maimai* and the climbing was over a track that was not really steep to the top where the going was level for a short way before a track bent down to the pool at the bottom of this basin-shaped depression. Whatever light we were getting on the upper ridges was gone. The pool and the hillsides near it were still black dark. A glance at my luminous watch showed six o'clock.

Setting out the decoys took only a few minutes as they are the kind that can be thrown out on the water where they right themselves and float naturally. I was neatly set in my *maimai* at 6.20; ten minutes to go before the legal starting time.

As usual I was in the fever of excitement that is the salt of my life. This was the first hour of the first day of the duck season. I was alone, unhampered and unworried by anything anybody else could do.

Ducks chattered overhead and their wings whistled as they swept by, turned and splashed down into the pool in blackness. Though it was after legal opening time I could see nothing. Another lot came in, but something scared them and the whole lot left with a roar of wings.

It was nearly seven o'clock before I could see the birds against the dark hillside. Three came in and I was rewarded with a right- and left-barrel kill. There is nothing in my world of hunting or fishing that can ever equal the thrill of that moment.

Although I pulled some rotten shots later and missed some easy shots, I did manage to collect my limit of ten ducks by 9.22 and only one had to be chased.

Though this was not the first time I'd shot my limit bag on the hillside pool, it was a most satisfactory one.

I was no longer to be scared of riding on Hector's tractor and never again did the old stump on the ridge look like a tombstone. And my "queer madness" was cured, at least for eleven months.

In a situation like the hillside pool where there is no current and no breeze of importance, the recovery of dead ducks from the surface of the water can be a real problem. I had learned that wading in such a place where the depth is unknown and the bottom is soft and muddy can be full of grief and woe. To obviate trouble it pays to carry as part and parcel of one's gear a couple of sixty-yard hapuka fishing lines. On this pool one only was quite long enough even when the pond was flooded, but on larger waters the two lines joined together can reach 120 yards.

To have proper control and possible full need of a line it *must* be absolutely anchored at one end. It needs no imagination to realise that under some circumstances on deep and rapid waters it could be a lifesaver. But for my game of recovery of the bag it is also important to anchor it properly. By walking around the pond it is child's play to engage the floating carcases and draw them gently out to the shore. If one misses a mark and the line slips over or under the bird the line is lifted and flipped backward like a skipping rope for another shot. The line is fully under control and, being well anchored at the other end, can be loosened or tightened at will.

Recovery of the decoys is even simpler and needs no explanation.

To keep the line in good order it should be wound up in such a way that the air can pass through it when it is hung up. If it has been used in sea-water it should be washed under a tap as soon as possible. The fellows who go sea fishing with a handline know exactly how all this is done. Their lines, like mine, will last a lifetime. As a good line can cost more than eight dollars this is something worth knowing.

Of course the man who is lucky enough to be able to own and keep a good gundog avoids problems of this sort.

19. Big Duck or Small Goose?

This is the paradise duck. Captain Cook, who could have been the first to see the bird, called it "Painted Duck". Somewhere, someone, called it "Paradise Duck"; and so it is likely to be for all time.

It took me a long time to discover that the paradise duck is the finest and most exciting game bird in New Zealand; and because I feel that this bird is virtually unknown to most of our duckshooters, I am hoping to help them to get the most out of this marvellous bird.

In my visits to Lake Hatuma, in Hawkes Bay, where I shot for some seasons with the Haldanes, one or two of these big ducks had fallen to my gun. The chances I had were just fortuitous and merely incidental to the duckshooting for which we were organised.

Quite unlike the ducks which would respond to the caller, a kind of little wooden trumpet which is blown in imitation of the cries of the wild duck, the paradise ignored the calls we then used, and they flew over our decoys more or less out of curiosity. I have never seen one alight on the water with the decoys as the grey duck will. I used to think that this might be due to their keener eyes detecting that the decoys were made or cork of canvas; it did not occur to me that it was because they were not ducks at all, but a kind of goose.

It was not until I started wildfowling in the King Country that I detected the fact that these birds congregated in communities out in open pasture lands, quite unlike ducks; and that they can land on, and take off from, the ground. It was only then I saw the real difference between them and the ducks.

But even then, I did not realise that shooting them in the open, away from water, was a possibility.

When I first shot at Mr Romayne's farm at Ohura I had a new look at the paradise. This was when my host came with me to stir up pukeko out of the swamp so I could get a shot at them. The pukeko had become too numerous for his liking and the nuisance had to be abated. When we reached the extreme boundary gate of his farm and were about to turn back, there was a flight of paradise ducks overhead, making a great fuss in their calling.

They alighted on a grassy ridge a few hundred yards from us.

That was the first lot. There must have been about a dozen. In a few minutes they set up more yelling and, with similar cries, another lot joined them. This was a wonderful moment for a birdwatcher. There in front of us were over twenty of the wild birds, some picking at the grass; some just standing there, watchful; a few with outstretched neck, chasing one another.

The build up of the gaggle continued. Sometimes only two or three birds circled the brow and each time the cries they gave were answered by reassuring replies from the ones on the ground. On and on the amazing scene developed, until there must have been seventy altogether. Suddenly, as though at a signal, the whole lot rose in the air and streamed away together in the direction whence they had come.

"Hector," I said to my friend, "that is the most remarkable sight I've ever seen. Where do they come from?"

"I think I know that," he answered with a smile. "Would you like a shot at them?"

"Most certainly; but they are *not* on the Auckland licence."

In the course of the year a suggestion was made to the Auckland Acclimatisation Society that paradise duck should be included on the licence. This was finally agreed to. The daily limit was fixed at five and was included in the usual duck limit of ten per gun per day.

One night after this amendment had become effective and I was again at the farm, my host rang a neighbour and arranged with him that I should have a day's shooting at the big birds. When I arrived on the scene, I was met at the woolshed by Mr McVicar. He had his gun with him so off we set at once over the first range to where there is a rather extensive stretch of swamp and pasture lying between two main ridges. From the top we could see a large community of paradise duck stirring restlessly. As soon as they spotted us they set up a chorus of high-pitched cries of warning and alarm, but did not rise.

Keeping out of sight we built a rough *maimai* under a mingimingi bush in the water. This meant standing in the water kneedeep, but this is a small matter to a duckshooter. Three of my painted decoys were stuck out, not in the water as in orthodox duck shooting, but on the grassy bank thirty yards away.

Mac then sneaked along the swamp, still keeping out of sight of the quarry. He made a wide circle to approach them from the far side.

Quite suddenly there was a chorus of alarmed screams from the flock immediately followed by the reports of the gun.

The air was filled with shrieking birds as they rose in a cloud and then broke in to smaller lots, scattering in all directions.

At least eight came my way climbing rapidly; they would have been out of range above me, but flattened out to pass my front at about forty yards. I got two shots away right and left. To my joy both birds turned over in the air and thudded to the ground. In about forty years of duckshooting in New Zealand, this was one of my greatest moments.

When Mac came back he had a female paradise which fell to his second barrel. His first shot had missed.

By this time the swamp was silent, all the birds had gone.

Well pleased, we sat out on the bank to have sandwiches and a drink. There, becoming better acquainted, we talked of our earlier days when limit bags of twenty-five were common. Then, without a sound, half a dozen of the birds flew right over us without seeing their danger. They took fright and turned back over the ridge. We had missed a good chance of a shot. Then it occurred to us that this was a sign that if we kept out of sight more might come our way.

After waiting an hour or so, sure enough, we heard cries from high above us. These must have spotted the dead ones on the bank where we had placed them, for they turned in a wide circle to come back for a closer look. Again Mac dropped one, a beautiful shot, and I got two down. One of mine got up and started to walk away. I made the mistake of declining my mate's offer to race after it. I thought I could do it myself, but was too slow, and it beat me into the raupo swamp whence only a good dog could have retrieved him.

Next season we shot together again using the same plan but not with the same success. My mind had not yet grasped the idea of a better technique. This was worked out after Lance Frost took over the management of the estate. Like Mac, he turned out to be a first-class mate and an excellent shot. We found that after the first shot or two the paradise did not like pitching back into the swamp pasture land, but preferred to light on a high ridge.

One or two would alight and when others flew near these were greeted with cries of welcome. Soon one lot after another joined the party. This seemed a regular pattern, like the build-up Hector and I had seen from his boundary gate five years earlier.

Lance and I decided to build a *maimai* up there. This sort of thing would cause the orthodox duckshooter to think we were crazy.

Floods or something prevented me from using the *maimai* the following season, although Lance and one of his sons had prepared it.

In 1964 we tested our plan. Hector came with me to assist. When we got to the woolshed Lance was all ready for us with his caterpillar tractor and steel-shod sledge. On to the sledge he had built a sedanlike chair at the back of which there were racks for guns and gear. Behind the chair was a platform for Hector to stand on. I felt like a rajah sitting there with arm rests to hang on to: I braced my feet against the corner struts of the sledge.

Storm water had scoured the tracks rather severely, but the caterpillar drive-belts made short work of getting over them. Until we got to the top not far from the *maimai* my body was subjected to all sorts of twists, jolts and jerks.

The *maimai* was really a dugout, a trench about four feet deep by two feet wide and about six feet long. Clumps of rushes and some tea-tree around the top made it a perfect hide. There was even a shelf dug at the end for a seat.

Would the birds come?

I set out the decoys on the slope facing the swamp. If they came my way at all they could not help seeing what I hoped they would mistake for their own kind.

It was easy to see why the shrewd geese (or ducks) favoured the crown of this ridge. It was a perfect observation post. Not even a rabbit could have moved down in the swamp without being detected by them. And certainly no man could have approached their landing ground unseen.

While we were setting out our decoys the big gaggles down below watched us with suspicion and stirred restlessly, all the time uttering their warnings to one another, but did not take to the air.

Lance Frost was a good enough stalker to walk away from them until he got out of their sight and then double back, cross the swamp to the far side and creep behind them. I could see him from my position, but they could not from theirs. When they became aware of his presence there was a hullabaloo of screams and yells as they took to the air. I saw two slight puffs of smoke and the reports came up to me. I saw nothing fall, but saw Lance sprinting along and over a ridge. Another shot was heard and he came in sight again carrying his kill.

I was so interested in all this byplay that I was caught napping by five which swept over my head. I called them with a goose call and they swung round and came back. My two shots appeared to have no effect whatever. They yelled madly and flew back towards the swamp. I watched them go with dismay. What had I done wrong? Concluding I had fired too far ahead of them through misreading their speed, I could only use appropriate words and feel a bit foolish.

By this time the swamp was silent. Not a bird was to be seen, in the air or anywhere else. The only consoling thought was that our plan of a hilltop *maimai* looked like being a success. It had worked with that lot in spite of the rough and ready decoys.

Soon Lance rejoined me and set up his dead one with the dummies. He told me that the two birds I had fired at had detached themselves from the other three, had gradually lost height and finally collapsed and fallen in the heart of a big patch of raupo and thick growth. There was no hope of retrieving them.

Now came the repetition of the birds returning. In lots of just a few to lots of twenty or so, they came back over their home at intervals of an hour to two or even more. Round and round they would go scanning the ground for their enemy. Once ten came in to land and got a hot reception before they could do so. We wound up the day with eight. Lance took his five—the day's limit per gun—and I killed three, so, with the two lost in the swamp, we could claim a double limit bag for the day.

All except one had fallen for the trick *maimai* built on the top of a hill.

It is no use flogging a dead horse, so it is just as futile growling about the paradise being called a duck. Dr Oliver, in his *New Zealand Birds* says Latham gave it the name of variegated goose. Gmelin converted this to Casarca variegata. Dr Oliver told me that he did not know who first dubbed it paradise duck.

So long as sportsmen are not fooled by its English name, and treat it, as we have found out how to do, as a landlubber rather than as a sailor, they can enjoy wonderful sport in its pursuit.

20. The Gun for the Job

The answer to the proposition—the gun for the job—has to be found by the shooting man himself. The first thing for him to realise, however, is that his success depends upon his finding the answer. Both man and gun have to suit each other and after that the man has to work out what he wants the gun to do for him. The "fit" of the gun is fairly simple to work out; and for the purpose he can do no better than to join a clay-bird gun club and enlist the interest of one of the members in his problem. He will get ready help from these people because all gun clubs desire new members and new converts to the rather expensive pastime. In short order he will learn safety rules for the handling of a firearm. There is no better school for the teaching of this important skill. He would be wise to select one man from whom to get advice about the length of the stock, the amount of cast off; the amount of bend that the stock should have, and such matters as balance and gun weight.

If he is to be a full time clay-bird shooter he must take heed of his club friend's advice regarding many other matters; but if he is just collecting gun wisdom which is to help his game shooting he could do worse than read this chapter.

The basic consideration of shotgun patterns is a thirty-inch diameter circle at 40 yards from the muzzle of the gun and the number of shot pellets registering hits on that circle. Gun men call this "the pattern" of a barrel.

The "standard" gun usually available in the gunshops in New Zealand is a hammerless double-barrelled 12-gauge with 30-inch barrels which are chambered to use $2\frac{3}{4}$-inch cartridges and bored half-choke for the right-hand barrel, which is usually fired first, and full-choke for the left barrel.

The gunstock is made so that the heel is set down about two and a half inches below a line drawn along the top of the barrels; it is also set half an inch to the right of this imaginary line. These two features are called "the bend" and "the cast off" and the degrees of bend and cast off are intended to suit the average man which, surprisingly enough, they do; though they can be a long way out for some.

A left-handed shooter—one who mounts the gun to his left shoulder—requires that the cast should be the opposite way to that of the gun in the shop.

These are the points of care that can be ironed out with the help of a gun-club friend. A knowledgeable shop man can be of great assistance when you can find one. The fit of the gun can be seen quickly by the assistant standing in front of the customer and making him raise the gun quickly and point it at his right eye. This is not a pleasant thing to do; and the assistant has to be keen on making a sale to do it. All the same he can see at once whether the mounted gun is lined up naturally at his own eye. If the gun is pointed too low it is because there is too much bend on the stock. If it is to one side then the cast is too much or not enough.

The prospective buyer must never be allowed to pull a trigger in this business even though everyone has made sure there is no cartridge in the breech. There is a case recorded in England of a firing pin point breaking in a test like this. The unfortunate instructor was struck by the tiny missile which entered the brain through the right eye.

Gun-fit can be gauged in another way when the user is by himself and there is no one to help him. It is this: He aims the gun at some small mark and then, but not until then, glances along the barrels. If the gun is a reasonable fit he will be "on" the mark.

He can do even better by setting up a target in a suitable spot, smudging something the size of a quail on it and firing without squinting along the barrel. He can soon see the result. The English gun trade makes a "try-gun"—an ingenious contraption with adjusting screws in the stock whereby the length of stock, bend and cast on or cast off can be altered to suit the customer. But in this case the customer is expected to order the gun to be made accordingly and is expected to wait for perhaps a year for the gun to be made. When it is, he can expect to be required to find quite a few hundreds of guineas to pay for it.

Even when our gentleman has his gun made to measurement he might still be a long way from having a gun that will fill the bag. And I now come to the real issue of the gun for the job.

Your gun-club friend will be heavily impressed with the virtue of good patterns. He knows that success on the clays depends upon a close pattern so that the clay is struck with as many pellets as possible or it might not get smashed even though an odd pellet has struck it. Another thing: The clay bird is a small target, especially when sailing edge on.

There cannot be any rule laid down as to the best size of shot pellet to use on duck and goose. It all seems to be a matter of choice for the gunner himself and his guide is his own personal shooting experiences. All the same, one can take the risk of suggesting that a goose needs to be hit by pellets as heavy as No 2 and not lighter than No 4. Duck sizes can be chosen according to the conditions generally met with by the user himself. Most men use the No 5 for the right barrel and No 4 for the left, though the demand for No 4 suggests that many use it all round.

A point to remember is that the larger the shot the farther its range for effectiveness; for instance, a No 3 shot pellet is given in the ballistics tables as being effective at 89 yards; No 4 at 79 yards; No 5 at 66 yards or a falling off of 10 yards per size. But it must also be kept in mind that the bigger the pellets the thinner the pattern becomes as the charge moves forward.

The proposition laid down by Askins is: "Shot in their forward motion do the killing, but patterns do the hitting." One pellet can kill a duck, but it must be an uncommon kill. It is this uncommon shot that accounts for the very long kills we hear about. They are flukes. By and large it takes three or four pellets of say No 4 to bring down a duck; each pellet having an energy at 40 yards of 4 lbs. Four pellets hitting the bird with an energy of 16 lbs should fetch him to the ground. There appears to be no end to the mathematics of shot-gun ballistics, so all we can do here is to consider soberly what we wish our gun to do.

The claybird marksman has no doubt in this respect. He wants a gun with close choke that will give him the minimum spread of pellets over the range. He knows that even a well-aimed shot can fail to break his small clay target if the pattern of his charge is thin enough to let his target sail on unbroken even though it might have been in the middle of his charge of pellets. Indeed this is the only way he can account for his misses!

So, except for skeet shooting, which is covered by a separate and distinct set of rules and conditions, the clay shooter wants the spread of his shot to remain "close" for the flight of the charge, as he is a good enough marksman, who has had much practice at the more or less stereotyped angles of flight, to miss but rarely.

But let us stick to our duck. He is the most important target for the vast majority of our shooters in New Zealand.

It is possible that the claybird shooters are practically all men who take out a licence to shoot wildfowl. We do not concern ourselves with these men. They are experts and do not need advice, and I am the last man to be presumptuous enough to offer it to them.

But, good and all as most of these men are, I have known cases where they have been helped to better scores on the Glorious First by easing up a bit on this full-choke idea.

One of these was Peter Hislop. We shot as fellow guests

at George Stratmore's farm on the edge of Wairarapa Lake, each in his own *maimai*. The shooting was quite good that year and we all did pretty well, that is to say, we all had a fair number of chances. It was all wing shooting. No one cared to shoot at the ducks on the water, though it was not then unlawful to do so, as it is now.

After the shoot was over, Peter came over to me and said: "I did some poor shooting this morning. Do you think my gun fits me? Some of those birds looked easy, yet I missed quite a few. I'd like your advice."

I had a look at the gun, which was of good make, as hammerless ejector models are, as a rule. The barrels were both bored full-choke.

I told Peter that I had been through the same kind of trouble in the Whangamarino swamps in 1931. That year I used a Greener hammerless trap model that was, like his, full-choke in both barrels. The "easy" shots (close) were nearly all missed. The seventeen that I bagged (the limit was then twenty-five) were nearly all fast high-flying birds passing almost right over my head.

Even after that experience I did not understand why the easy shots were missed and the difficult ones were successful on that dark wet morning. It was some months later, when I read an article in an American paper by Captain Curtis of *Field and Stream* who wrote: "One can be easily deceived in the darkish dawn with flighting ducks. They are closer than they appear to be, and one needs an open-bore gun, throwing a wide pattern, to have a chance."

I took the matter up with Charlie Saunders our gunsmith who had no doubts about the matter: "What you want, Mr Kelly, is a "driven-game" gun for those close shots. In the Old Country we had to make guns in pairs for our customers. One gun for the butt with cylinder bore in the right and modified choke, or just improved cylinder in the left. The other gun is for 'walk-up' shooting in the field. To try to kill birds at short range, say 20 to 30 yards with full-choke gun is silly. It's either miss or (shocking) mincemeat."

That was the end of the matter. The following season I had a light Midland gun with 28-inch barrels that were bored improved cylinder and modified choke. It was completely satisfactory.

My friend Peter took his gun to Archie Caldwell who very reluctantly opened the right barrel for him, but before doing so, sent for me: "You know I hate doing this," he said. "It's spoiling a good gun." Though he grumbled about it, he did the job, as he did everything, thoroughly.

The sequel was so satisfactory to Peter that he has since had a gun of high quality made to the same boring specification for his future duck and pheasant shooting.

To wind up the message contained in the foregoing lines I should like to add that I purchased a Watson ejector doublebarrelled hammerless in 1946 and have used it with satisfaction every season since. It is bored for driven game.

If we break away from the double-barrelled gun and use an auto-loader or a hand-operated repeater, we can have a gadget fitted to the muzzle that allows an "at will" variation to the choke. This is a popular gun with many men as they can have any degree of choke they wish. All that is needed is to turn the outer case of the poly-choke gadget to give any desired degree. It can be done between shots in a moment.

21. Dawn Watch for the Canada

When I realised, at last, that Paradise ducks were geese in everything but name, and when I learned how they should be hunted, I felt that I had found the ultimate in New Zealand feathered game. As far as the North Island is concerned this seems a fair enough opinion. But I had reckoned without the Canada Goose (*Branta canadensis*) of the South Island.

Much has been written about this introduced bird. A good deal of enthusiasm about its successful introduction and acclimatisation withered in the hot blasts from pastoralists who demanded its extermination because it ate grass and fouled pastures.

As a result of the uproar, geese were removed from the list of birds regarded as game and, as such, protected by law for the greater part of the year. Because of this degraded status I had overlooked the Canada goose as a game bird.

The situation is not as bad as I thought; I find that he is still game in Waimate, Waitaki and North Canterbury acclimatisation districts. He is therefore still subject to controlled shooting.

The Canada was brought back to my notice sharply by a film that was exhibited in Taupo by Allan Hall, assistant conservator (Rotorua) of the wildlife division of the Internal Affairs Department. This was a nature film entitled "A Place to Live". The scene is Lake Ellesmere in North Canterbury, and it was photographed by Peter Morrison of the wildlife division.

Among the star actors was the Canada goose. Mr Hall gave a knowledgeable commentary on various aspects of the picture as he projected it, telling us, among other things, that the film had won for its maker a valuable bursary from the British Broadcasting Corporation.

All kinds of bird life in Lake Ellesmere are shown in the film, with details of nest building, hatching and rearing of chicks. Perhaps the shyest and most vigilant bird shown is the Canada goose. Peter Morrison achieved the almost impossible when he recorded the intimate details of its family life. While we, my wife and I, were entranced by this wonderful film of New Zealand bird life, it seemed to us that the great Canada goose stole the show. We determined that we would go down to Lake Ellesmere district as soon as possible so that we could watch the birds for ourselves.

Early one March we drove south and were duly and most efficiently landed from the car ferry *Aramoana* at Picton, and from there went on to Kaikoura where we spent the night. We drove on next day along the dramatic coast of crashing combers and black broken rocks to Christchurch. There we spent a few days of intense activity, finally escaping to Southbridge where we were welcomed by Mr and Mrs Dunn of Southbridge Hotel who looked after us excellently and assisted us with information that was most helpful. To them and to Mr and Mrs Duncan Lockhead of Southbridge we are grateful for the success of our visit and the observations we made of the bird life of the lake and its surroundings.

Next morning I was awake at 4.20 and dressed in bush woollens. By five I was warmed and comforted with tea and toast in Mrs Dunn's cheerful and immaculate kitchen.

It was pitch black outside, with chilly drizzling rain, when I headed the Cortina for Taumotu, Fisherman's Point, the timber yards, or anywhere else where geese were to be expected. I was madly early, of course. Not knowing the area, I just followed my headlights until I found myself among small cottages and huts. A shore strewn with nets, eel traps, upturned boats and other fishing things stopped me. I waited but a minute or so, then turned and groped back until I reached a side road leading right. This, I felt, would take me parallel to the lake, but I was unsure of my position.

Then I was at a cross-roads, and knew instinctively that this was a place to wait!

It was still drizzling but light was growing in the high sky. I could see fences, and made out a light dray standing, apparently deserted, in a paddock. It evoked memories of a farm boyhood when we learned to yoke horses to a dray like it: winkers first, collar, hemes, saddle, girth—not too tight— get the traces even length; fasten the breechings last, keep those reins clear. No two horses the same.

There was Coley, who would bolt at the first chance; there was Blossom, "Fatarse" when the girls were not there. She was as gentle as a lamb. There was Ding, the old devil, who would kick and bite. There the first rule was kindness to all animals.

I was jerked back to the present by the cry of a bird from the dark sky. "Er Hunk, Er Hunk"—the unmistakable call of a wild goose though I had never heard it before.

Excitedly I jumped out of the car, binoculars in hand. The cry came nearer, and then I saw a large bird flying at a great height in a semi-circle above me. He was alone and was, I judged, a pilot. He turned back towards the sea and disappeared. I had heard and seen my first wild goose.

Within minutes more cries came out of the still murky sky, this time from a point farther north. I could see nothing and the calls were coming from several birds. Suddenly I saw a long, dark, ragged line of geese flying at about 1,500 feet. They looked astonishingly like an irregular smudge of black smoke as they moved inland. It was difficult to credit that this cloud was made up of living creatures, but there they were!

This was the real thing. This was the spectacle of which Peter Scott has written, and to see which he travelled many times across perilous seas even as far north as the Arctic Circle.

And yet this glorious sight was mine for so small an effort. The cloud of geese drew closer and their calls formed a chorus of notes from the skies.

Even as I watched, a section of the cloud broke off and, to my joy, the birds set their wings in that fixed position waterfowl use when they want to come down. I counted the dark forms and saw that there were twelve of them. They were pitching at an angle earthwards that would bring them almost to my feet. Down, down, down. All as one, their cries now seemed to be conversational. Surely, I thought, they are telling each other what they see below.

In desperation I dashed the water off my spectacles. I grabbed the camera, and getting the group in the vision square pressed the shutter. To have recorded that picture of that group of Canada geese with their great wings held down with feet stretched forward to take the shock, tails and head bent in sympathy, would have given me more joy than if I could have bagged the lot. I knew it was impossible in the light against the dark sky for the picture to register, but I just had to try.

So the only picture I have is in my treasure house of memories where it will remain as one of the most thrilling scenes of wildfowl that I have ever known.

Most wonderfully the flight ended in a stubble field 150 yards from where I stood by the car.

As I watched more and still more lowered themselves out of the mists musically to join "my" pilot gaggle. Soon I lost count as the community grew to hundreds until I could only guess at 500 of them.

In better light I watched them through binoculars. They were gleaning some sort of food from that stubble field. The birds flew along steadily, pecking and pecking at the ground. Some few were standing stock-still with heads raised like sentinels. Others just seemed to squat down with necks outstretched. Were these a listening post? The whole side-view could have been mistaken as a flock of newly shorn lambs which had been exposed to a storm of reddish brown dust.

The morning show was over. I found myself wet and chilled as I climbed back into the car. I switched on the lights, started the engine and drove quietly away. As far as I could see the birds stayed where they were, though I guessed all heads were raised in vigilance. So I left them in peace.

Our friends had advised us to go down to the mouth of the Selwyn River. In spite of the weather, the two of us set off after breakfast. It was about twenty miles from our hotel. I was anxious that Truda should see the Canada geese at close range and hear their ringing cry.

We passed through a collection of small buildings that are known as the Selwyn huts, noticing at the same time that many were worthy of a higher name. As far as we could see, they were all vacant. Without pausing, we drove along a slimy, waterlogged driveway as far as we dared. Then, gum-booted and in waterproofs, we stumped across the soggy, mossy salt-marsh towards the lake edge.

Dark lines of birds seemed to be drawn up along the shore. In the drizzle and murk even a pair of good binoculars gave us only moderate visual aid, but we were able to make out scores and scores of swans and geese, with small groups of ducks keeping a respectful distance from the bigger birds.

On the sands we saw the white breasts of gulls.

The light was hopeless for photography although attempts had to be made; the results were no better than could be expected.

We used whatever cover we were able to find for our advance, but there was not much available. We paused on the inland side of a large uprooted tree stump. Whichever way we looked to the north or south, the shore line was alive. Swans and geese for the most part, then ducks and seabirds. It was an amazing sight.

As we gazed across this scene of sodden desolation at that

black line we knew that there was faint hope that any would take the air in our direction. Rather, it seemed to me more likely that the flights, if any, would be in the other direction. Suddenly there was a faint sound from the mists behind us. Then two Canada geese were flying right over us not fifty feet up. The "Er Hunk, Er Hunk" of their passing was the first time Truda had heard the call. She was thrilled, as I was, to see these two so close and in flight.

"Oh, Kelly. Aren't they exciting," she gasped. "Oh, the lovely things!!"

"Yes. They are," I heard myself saying absently. I was thinking of something else.

Those two birds were well within gunshot. How did it happen they didn't see us?

I can only conclude that the Canada, for all his wisdom, can make a mistake occasionally. These two had offered perfect left and right shots. Their flight was unbroken and it was clear they had not seen us. Their arrival at the water set up the usual gaggle of welcome.

Nothing else happened along, so we continued our slow move forwards. But the birds were not pleased with our visit, as they demonstrated very clearly, by rafting out to sea at the same rate. If we stopped, so did they; as we went forward again, the rafts moved away at the same slow pace. We were getting nearer the water, but not a whit closer to our wild friends.

A few lots of ducks took off on short flights along the shore, but the geese and swans just retired in good order and with dignity farther and farther away. They kept about 200 yards of no-man's land and water between us. It was both frustrating and amusing. Finally we gave up and returned to the car for our sandwiches and hot drinks.

We did get closer views of the Canada in the afternoon when Mrs Duncan Lockhead took us on an observation tour. We saw numbers of many kinds of water-birds on this run of about fifty miles. Wildlife refuges have been established and it was at these that we found the birds less afraid. But even though our views were closer, the weather still made picture-taking a waste of time.

It is our ambition to return to the home of this wonderful goose; to see him again when the day is being born beneath a clear sky and he comes in his smudgy-black ragged rabbles to swoop from his half-mile-high airways to his breakfast on the field of an unwilling host.

And it would be a great treat to meet him again on the beautiful waters which he has chosen as "A Place to Live".

22. *Kaimanawa Mountains*

Perhaps when a man has passed his seventy-seventh year he should be content to sit under a pepper tree and mumble with old professor Arnold Wall:

> "Happy the faithful, they who fill
> With mountain memories, stored away,
> With hauntings and high ecstasies
> All the waste corners of their day."

But I can't see it that way. So when I was offered a trip by helicopter into the heart of the wild Kaimanawas to see how venison hunters worked, it was too good a chance to miss.

The beginning of this adventure, if such it can be called, was my unending search for game meat for the household cat. For the first eight years of his active life Smutty had had the choicest fare: venison, rabbit, hare, goat, wild pork—and he knew the difference from butcher's pork—opossum and fresh trout from the river.

From tiny kittenhood, when he travelled in the pocket of an old Harris tweed sports coat, he ruled Mar Lodge and its twenty acres as lord and master; and when I say this I mean that the owners were, to him, his loyal and grovelling subjects.

Because he was black, with only six white hairs on his chest, he was named Smuts. As he developed he became restless and relentless in his pursuit of his own wild meat, choosing young rabbits before all else. These he would trot home with and bring to me to be cleaned and skinned. He must have killed hundreds of them. A fully grown one I saw him with was rather more than three-quarters dead. He had dragged it as far as the old cowbails with only a hundred yards to go. Smuts was nearly as dead as the rabbit. Stoats and weasels were common enemies. These he dragged home and laid in the middle of the lawn.

At that time I had bought a new Brno ·22 repeating rifle to which I added a telescopic sight. It was, and still is, a deadly accurate weapon and accounted for so many of the grey pests that they became scarce on the paddocks.

After this Field-Marshal Smuts would send me fishing, and would watch me go down the track to the stream. On my return he would be sitting at the top of the track to greet me. If a fish had been caught, he would demand his share forthwith—and generally got it. Though there was plenty of venison Smutty soon tired of this, so something else had to be found. He would catch mice until he skinned them out around the house and sheds; rats—and he was rough on rats—were not in his line as tucker. If necessary, I would take out the car and drive across the Whakapapa and shoot a rabbit or two; at the worst I'd have to drive six miles to the nearest butcher's shop for some "people's meat", that is, the best.

You can gather from this, the sort of trouble we were in when we sold Mar Lodge and returned to Wellington. The old warrior cried all the way there in the car in spite of being nursed on my wife's lap. No game meat was possible in Wellington, so the best "people's meat" had to be provided for him. Sea fish was very well received and for a while all went well enough. Once when we were short, a tin of patent cat-food was opened. The scorn with which this was rejected was terrible; we did not make that mistake again, ever.

Finally when we found that city life was dust and ashes in our mouths, we sold the big house and hastened back to the beautiful King Country with its lovely rivers and friendly people. Smutty sat up in the car like Jacky as happy as the king he was, knowing full well that we had "had" city life for all time as well as he had.

But again we were forced to change; as life for me a thousand feet above sea-level is essential, we came to Taupo. Here we have trout, but game flesh for Smutty was still elusive. It was at this lucky moment that I found Bill Hindmarsh and his venison works. For a time all was well again, but Bill got interested in another line of business.

Then one day I saw in a Taupo street a sign "River Ridge Game Meat Company". I walked in. The shop was a large one equipped with all the usual things, such as scales and hooks, counters and telephones. There was not a scrap of meat in sight. A young man came forward from the rear premises wearing the usual blue and white apron and equipped with a businesslike knife.

"Have you any hares?" I asked him.

"Yes."

"Do you have them as a rule?"

"Yes." He produced one frozen as hard as a brick, but skinned and quartered. He weighed it carefully.

"Seven and a penny, sir."

It was then I asked the silly question:

"River Ridge. That's a funny name to call a shop. I always thought rivers ran along valleys, not ridges."

"Oh. Well you see, my name is Ridge and my partner's is Rivers."

After this exchange I made many visits to the game shop and in the course of time I was admitted to the operating theatre where the carcasses of game are dealt with. The deer are brought there headless and gutted. The carcasses are skinned and cut up to the appropriate sections encased in plastic bags, packed in cartons and quick frozen.

Hastings Air-Road Services carry the parcels to the Farmers' Freezing Co. in Auckland, which, in turn, ships venison to Hamburg, Germany and Marseilles, France; hares and pork to Genoa and Dunkirk.

K

In this spotlessly scrubbed room it was usual to see three or four men hard at work skinning, trimming and packing. But, though there might be ten to twenty carcasses on the gambrels, I have never yet seen any sign of fly-strike. How do they manage this?

Every hunter knows very well that when he shoots a deer, the blowflies get there before he can. He knows that by the time he has gralloched the carcass or skinned off the cape and head, the busy flies have deposited their larvae on exposed flesh and around the eyes and mouth. Given time they will build small mats of larvae on the outer pelage. Then how the devil did these meat hunters manage to keep the flies off?

One day I asked Mr Rivers the question. He must, by this have decided that the best way to silence me was to say:

"Would you like to go up to the camp with Goodwin in his helicopter? You can see for yourself. We expect the helicopter will be ready very soon." And he added: "The boys would be thrilled to see you up there. Go as our guest. You would be sure to get a story out of it for your new book."

The offer left me rather breathless. What a lark it would be! I accepted on the spot.

It was some months before I made the trip, and then it was not in the helicopter but in Goodwin McNutt's Taylercraft, a game little single-engined fixed winger.

So it came about that, because of Smuts's passion for wild meat, I have had two quite unexpected trips into two of the most interesting fishing and shooting places in the mountains.

Nervously I outlined the project to my wife. She rose to it with:

"It would be wonderful for you. You must go. I'll make you a cake."

Twice the cake was made; twice was the date postponed.

"Next time the date is fixed I'll give you a packet of gingernuts," she said. But one day I had a ring:

"Can you be ready at ten in the morning?"

A few minutes later I heard the cakemixer going.

Mr Rivers called at my home in Taupo with his truck at the appointed time and we were away, cake and all. It was a perfect morning. Half an hour later we were at the Rangitaiki Hotel, which stands as a centre of social life and fount of information to a wide expanse of thirsty-looking plain. It is therefore an oasis of sustenance where no man need suffer the pangs of frothless thirst for very long.

There was not a soul in sight as we approached the buildings but, when we entered by a door, that was easily explained. We discovered the entire population of the district, or so it seemed. Our entry passed unnoticed. Mr Rivers bought some cigarettes or tobacco for the boys at camp, but I did not notice anything I wished to purchase at that moment. A few hundred yards away we stopped on the airstrip, where we were soon joined by Mr McNutt in his plane. It appeared at first in a "V" in the range as a small black speck and even when it touched down as gently as a bird and taxied up to the truck, it still looked a tiny thing.

Out of it stepped a tall lithe man, Goodwin McNutt himself, of whose daring as a bush pilot I had heard so much. At once he started to pull out of the cabin carcass after carcass of sika and red deer. I felt one; it was as cold as though it had come from a cool-room, a pretty good hint as to what I could expect in a tent at 4,000 feet that night.

In short order the seven carcasses of venison were loaded on the truck and I was shoehorned into my seat on the plane and strapped in, with my sleeping-bag, fishing rod, summat to eat and drink packed around me, and a rifle between my knees.

I have flown in many kinds of aircraft, but this was the smallest. Goodwin hopped into his seat, adjusted his belt, checked with obvious care and we were off like a bird. I felt ashamed of all the gear I had lugged along and was glad that there was no complaint from the pilot.

In a matter of minutes we were looking down on the wide and many coloured plains with their sharply defined blotches of browns, greens, yellows of tussock and white patches of bare pumice. Odd shiny pieces were probably swampy waterholes; black patches the shadows of the few clouds in the sky.

The little engine of the Taylercraft roared away confidently as we gained greater height. Soon we flattened out and skimmed the highest ridges of the dividing range, then swept swiftly down one of the deep gorges, turning right or left as required. For miles the great beech forest lay wrinkled and twisted below us. I thought: "Down there is the home of the only herd of sika deer in the Dominion." Cervus sika nippon is, as his name suggests, the Japanese variety. The hunters call him "the Jap" and respect him for his skill in the forest and his cunning in evasion. That green forest looked from the air so tightly woven it seemed impossible that daylight could get through it. The edges of the forest were sharply cut as though trimmed with giant clippers; the snowgrass mats tucked neatly against the deep green of the forest quite unlike anything I had ever seen. That was the pattern, beech forest and snowgrass, the former always capping the tops and the latter apparently trying to push the forest higher and higher.

In the deep, deep gorges thin lines of water showed here and there. These traced where the waters gathered in the smaller gullies, each streamlet joined others and gaining volume and strength. This was the beginning of the Tauranga-Taupo River, I was told later, the river that is famed in song and story wherever trout fishermen get together. The pilot seemed to notice my interest and swung the craft round so that I saw another stream running with us, whereas the Tauranga-Taupo fell away behind.

The new river I guessed to be the Ngaruroro flowing east to Hawkes Bay.

Thousands of acres of snowgrass or tussock land stretched away downstream. The earth below resembled a ploughed field. The plane shuddered once or twice and then dived steeply towards the earth. Circling a few times it gave me the chance to spot a small camp. We dived again towards it and, it seemed flattened out only at the very last second. I felt a gentle bump or two as we touched down at the airstrip that I had not even seen. There we were within a few yards of the airsock, yellow and bellying in the breeze.

Two of the hunters greeted us, Peter and Ray. We were more than welcome, as the men were getting worried over some items of food. The gear was quickly unloaded from around my person and I was able to get out of the machine. I looked at my watch; it was only twenty-two minutes since we lifted off the airstrip at Rangitaiki. Experts calculate tramping time through the trackless dense forest and across crumpled open country, as anything up to a week between the same two points.

Goodwin McNutt had been flying in and out of this hunting area for ten years. He did not tell me, but I understand that the first time he just circled round what he judged to be a level spot in the snowgrass and landed! The tale goes that he had to clear away quite a bit of tussock and monowai brush before he could take off.

The camp consists of a large cooking-living tent of stout canvas and built on a sturdily constructed pole frame. The rear part is provided with an inner tent where the hunters sleep on a pile of snowgrass straw. They all sleep side by side; they never fall out.

Another and smaller tent had a camp bunk for one and this was allotted to me. The bed was quite comfortable though for one reason or another I called it Uneven Stevens. In my tent was a pile of reserve supplies or iron rations and two cases of ammunition. The amount of ammunition was impressive. Over my tent there was a big fly of heavy green canvas. Again I was struck by the strength that was built into the framework. I was to learn the reason for this a few days later.

Alongside my tent there was a store-room for the horse fodder. This was not so sturdily constructed, but built much as campers usually build in the open. The whole outfit was located in a donga about ten feet below the level of the plain. A rivulet of icy spring water flowed along the back of the camp; I, who had used the incomparable water from the glacier-fed Whakapapa, enjoyed once again this gift of the mountains.

Goodwin then showed me the coolroom where the carcasses are stored pending his airlift to the works. It consists of two rooms which are served with one exterior door, though the spare room had a heat-insulated door of its own.

The whole construction, if it could be so called is simply a dugout, or, as the Americans call it, a hogan. Opposite the tents is a steep bank of the donga, and the men dug their rooms straight into the bank. Here they have fashioned a flyproof wall in such a way that there is a constant current of cool air passing through and around the carcasses which are hanging on gambrels from stout poles in the roof. Even when the sun was blazing outside I stood in the hogan and was cooled past the point of comfort. There were blowflies buzzing round outside but not a single one inside. Once the meat is placed in the dugout it is perfectly safe. But how do the hunters get it from the hills? The answer emerged quite simply without a single question.

There were five or six carcasses on the hooks. They were headless, gutted and with lower joints of the legs removed. Each was spread open by a 12-inch wooden rod so that air passed through the cavities. A weighing machine was suspended from the roof, for the men were paid according to weight.

A corral fence ran round the open side of the donga; on the rails were draped the saddlecloths, horse covers and saddles. A neat pile of cut firewood was stacked against the fence. I was struck with the scrupulous tidiness of the corral and around the hitching rail. Even where the wood had been chopped, the area was raked clean.

After we had drunk tea Peter guided me to the nearest

fishing pool. Here I was to have a quite new fishing experience. It was surprising to find that the cold, clear hurrying water ran between banks that were bare of any kind of growth. I looked in vain for any fly or other sort of insect life. What was the use of trying to catch trout with artificial flies where no naturals that I could see existed? It wasn't. I tried everything in the way of fly-casting, in and over beautiful stretches; I waded in the ice-cold stream until muscles started to niggle with cramp. I gave it up. There were fish to be seen. Good ones of four or five pounds, but they just would not open their mouths for me. Afterwards on our sad trek campwards Peter said to me:

"You know, Mr Greg, those trout go only for spoon." And, as I am not a hurler of hardware, those trout can stay in their wonderful waters. If and when I return I intend to try a hairy nymph on them. They might mistake it for a mouse!

About midafternoon the hunters started to get ready for their day's work. Peter and his mate Ray rode off to the hills. Goodwin had flown away to his home at Waipukurau. Noel, the third hunter, we had not yet met. He was still out in the bush where he'd been all night, so I was left alone with my notebook and pencil.

You will already have found the answer to my query as to how the blowflies were beaten. The deer are shot in what an Irish friend of mine calls "the glow of the evening" and are in the cooler before daylight. Sometimes the shooting is done by electric spotlight, but this did not happen when I was there, as the battery was flat.

Knowing the men would be late back, I cooked their dinner from the abundant supplies now on hand. Peter came in at a quarter to nine; Noel and Ray just before ten. The thumps outside the dugout indicated to me that their trips had not been in vain. Seven carcasses was the immediate bag; Noel had left four more hanging in the bush to be retrieved in the early hours. After breakfast, which the youngest man prepared, the hunters collapsed. Not an eyelash moved for hours. I heard Noel recount his night's experience thus:

"It was cold, eh. About an inch and a half of snow, eh. Not much room on the little shelf and it's not level . . . nearly slipped into the river once, eh. Glad when it got light."

Then, a few minutes later:

"Could have got four more only for old Treacleface (the pack animal) he musta thought we were too far ahead. He let out a load whinny, eh. And next thing four Japs jumped and were gone before I could do a thing, eh."

It interested me that Noel did not seem to mind the cold that he must have suffered, saying merely: "It was cold, eh." I was in a good tent, with my sleeping-bag inside of which the kindly Peter had pushed a hotwater bottle, and placed a folded blanket over my feet. I was warm and comfortable, but Noel seemed to have nothing but a blanket and a heap of snowgrass under his sheet of calico on that night of hail and snow. "It was cold, eh," was a masterly understatement.

23. Snowgrass Country

I stayed with the hunters for several days during which I filled three exercise books with notes on this strange environment. On one of these days Mr Bob Tremaine, who shares the airstrip with Goodwin, called and the boys invited him to have morning tea. He told me that there was a cabin, or hut, built up in the forest above the camps; that it was used by shepherds and occasional visitors, and that one of the latter, Lester Masters, had written some stories in the visitors' book, that were worth reading.

At this point of the range there is a high upthrust of volcanic rock. It is a most striking feature and dominates the whole area. The peak is called Boyd Rock and the hut is also known as Boyd's. It seems that two brothers of this name tried to sheep-farm the area, but the big depression or slump, at the end of the 1920s, killed the brave enterprise. The remaining Boyd walked off the place leaving behind him two thousand sheep which were not shorn for two years. Traces of the disaster are still to be seen. I came across two dead longtails. Perhaps they had died of age or, as suggested by one of the hunters, shepherds had shot them, as they are not considered of value.

I climbed up to the Boyd Rock next day and found the hut. It is a large one built on a frame of birch poles. The floor is of earth and very bumpy. There is a huge galvanised iron fireplace opposite the door. Sack bunks "adorn" two walls, one tier above the other. Not a scrap of firewood nor rations could be found. An awfu' puir welcome. Ironically, there is a beer bottle suspended from the roof on a string. This is the dinner gong!

On the table was a case made of tin. It had a sliding metal lid. Inside was the visitors' book. The first entry was a typed sheet by Lester Masters, poet of the open country.

> "Please write down plain what you have seen;
> Tell of the muster or the chase,
> The luck you've had, and where you've been.
> Then park the book back in its case;
> So, that mabbe, when some man's son
> Comes drifting in from vale or spur
> He'll read what you have seen or done, —
> When you were here in days that were."

In spite of this plea, there is not a single hunting story recorded in the book except one or two which were written by Lester Masters himself. These are very interesting.

I had a closer look at the bush which crowns the hills and ridges. It is a type of nothofagus beech. Where I was the forest was open enough to get through without effort though there was a very thick mat of leaf and twig matter on the ground that made long walks tiring on the leg muscles. It was also no easy matter to move about without making considerable noise.

I spent some time poking round in the beech forest where I gathered some alpine plants for my wife's rockery.

On my return down to the plateau I called over to see the lodge Tremaine and Hall were building for their visitors. I was glad to meet Jim Hall who is a well-known deerstalker with many good trophies to show for his years of devotion to the sport.

The hunters were all gone from camp when I got back there. Knowing they would not be back until after dark, I prepared the evening meal. This time it was venison cooked very slowly in pineapple juice and served with tomato sauce and onions. It turned out to be a success.

The first hunter in was Noel with a heavy sika carcass on his saddle. After he had attended to the carcass and the needs of his horse, he came into the tent and joined me. Slowly the story came:

"This was a cunning fellow. Though he could not see me, he knew I was there somewhere. He kept moving away, turning his head in my direction. It took me nearly an hour to get a shot and I had to crawl a long way for it. He was trying all the time to make out what I was up to so that he could make his move. It was like a game, eh. In the end I saw him clearly and got my sights on him. I reckoned it about three hundred; a long shot, eh, but got him fair and square."

I told Noel that I knew very few who could have pulled that shot off successfully. He did not reply.

The silence lasted so long that it began to worry me. Would he think I doubted his story?

Suddenly he burst out:

"This is my last season slaughtering deer. This stag was a beautiful thing to watch and I had to admire the clever way he tried to keep out of danger. In the bush I'd have had no chance whatever, but the snowgrass was too low."

I waited. This was one of those rare moments when a New Zealand bushman speaks from the heart:

"I'm glad to find you by yourself, Mr. Kelly. I've killed deer for years. At Porouni station I killed 1,100 alone. But these little Japs. . . . They're graceful dainty things. I'm sick of killing them."

Again the silence while I waited:

"I just wanted to tell you," was all he added.

"What will you do?" I asked.

"I'll go back to batten splitting; it pays, and I don't mind the hard work."

Peter came in with two reds which were quickly gambrelled and made safe. We had our meal, the hunters saying how good it was to have one ready when they came in late at night.

I thought what a pleasant job it would be for some lone

man who was past his period of regular work, to camp-cook for men like these. He would get his food as well as companionship, and might be paid a moderate amount. If he were used to camping, with some knowledge of cooking, it would benefit the hunters as well as himself.

This night we were all in bed when the youngest hunter came in about eleven o'clock. I heard him arrive at the dugout. There was only one thump, so knew that he had only one kill. He had to make the best meal he could out of what had been left. Camp cooks never advertise "Meals at all hours".

Silence soon fell, and with it I was asleep on the instant that I zipped my sleeping-bag shut. I was jerked awake in what seemed a few minutes later, by an explosion. For a confused moment I was sure that an earthquake was the cause, but there was no movement in my bunk while everything else seemed to be trying to go somewhere and was shrieking with rage. Almost at once my mind grasped that it was a dry storm of great force. Though we were down in a donga, and the tents were built, as I had remarked earlier, with great strength, it seemed impossible that any tent could stand up to a storm like this. I looked at my watch; it was 2.20.

"Forty more minutes of danger, Greg," I heard myself mutter. "You know all the tents that have ever blown down on you, and one of them weighed down to the ground with snow, did so at three o'clock in the morning. So you have now, say, thirty-eight minutes to get through."

My soliloquy seemed to call extra blasts that should have blown the tent to pieces. A horse stamped and whinnied loudly almost at my head. I heard the tent next door go crashing down and some loose sheets of iron hurtling. That was the fodder tent, but empty. I had lashed my doorflap with strips of flax and wondered how much longer the canvas could stand that shrieking pressure. But Goodwin's foresight and hard work in the building of that camp, the stout quality of the new canvas, and the wisdom of using the natural shelter of the donga, were amply justified and rewarded. Silently I thanked the man who, helped by his wife, had carried those heavy frame poles out of the bush.

Shortly after the fodder tent had been wrecked I became aware that the storm had passed its peak and was abating. I fell asleep again.

When daylight came the golden tops of tussocks rippled and danced into focus. I watched fascinating "races" of this, New Zealand's most beautiful grass, as the easing winds turned the tresses left and right as though they were bowing in the day.

At 5.30 a plane roared in over the camp. It was not Goodwin's expected Taylercraft, but an Auster piloted by Bob Tremaine. My camp-mates must have recognised the sound of the plane, as no one stirred. Goodwin had apparently got caught up in his farming affairs in Hawkes Bay and was unable to leave them.

Mr Tremaine, knowing I was worried about my wife's anxiety because I had not returned on due date, kindly offered to fly me out when he could get the opportunity. This came the following day rather unexpectedly. It had been too boisterous during the afternoon and I had more or less given up hope when Bob called me from the top of the ridge: "If this wind drops a bit more by six I'll fly you home."

We met at the airstrip on time and there was an exciting minute or two while we waited for the airsock to steady in the right direction. Bob Tremaine was taking no unnecessary chance. I noticed that, like McNutt, he checked all the controls several times.

Then, at a signal to his partner Jim Hall, who was hanging on to the tail, he gave the engine the gun and we were committed to the take-off. We were soon in the air in that delightful lifting motion that must be as exhilarating to the pilot as it is to his passenger.

The tents fell away below, the silver winding thread of the river glinted for a few seconds and was gone as the machine spiralled to reach height enough to clear the top of the range.

"Do you get airsick?" Bob asked.

I reassured him on the point. How could a fellow get sick at such a thrilling time?

Glad as I was to be in the air on the way home, I was a bit disappointed that Goodwin had not been able to return to fly me into his select hunting area—the Northern Arm. The hunters had spoken about this valley with an impressive awe.

In the Auster we sat side by side so conversation was easy. Impulsively I asked, "Where is the place they call the Northern Arm, Bob?"

"I'll fly you over it," he offered generously and turned the plane sharply right and dived down across a ridge or two until we were over an open snowgrass valley tucked in neatly between the clean-cut edges of deep green forest. Flying quite low, Bob pointed to a small building against the forest. "That's Goodwin's," he said. A mere glance at the country below was enough to stir any hunter to his depths.

"Oh, to be down there, Bob!"

"Yes, it's a great spot. Now I'll show you our pet spot, Te Whakao. It resembles Northern Arm somewhat."

The engine roared as the pilot banked his machine to the left climbing rapidly. After flying west for a matter of ten minutes, Bob dropped to lower levels over another snowgrass valley. Here the country looked more settled with clearer ridges. A permanent camp of several cabins was built not far from bush on the southern side.

"When we can't fly in here, we can get through by Land-Rover from the main highway between Taupo and Turangi. Both red deer and sika here."

The plane swung north again off the beech country over grassland and tea-tree scrub. "That's the Hinemaiaia stream. American brook trout there. Next one is Waitahanui. Must let my wife know I'll be home for dinner."

He circled a group of houses, flew over the town of Taupo and came down gently to the runway.

"Thank you, Bob, for a thrilling ride over some exciting country," I said.

Now I keep thinking about the breezes rippling the gold tresses of the snowgrass and the keenness of the air in the early dawn up there in the mountains, and I am longing to go back, but I have to realise that a writer's work cannot always be done the play-way.